essentials

essentials liefern aktuelles Wissen in konzentrierter Form. Die Essenz dessen, worauf es als „State-of-the-Art" in der gegenwärtigen Fachdiskussion oder in der Praxis ankommt. *essentials* informieren schnell, unkompliziert und verständlich

- als Einführung in ein aktuelles Thema aus Ihrem Fachgebiet
- als Einstieg in ein für Sie noch unbekanntes Themenfeld
- als Einblick, um zum Thema mitreden zu können

Die Bücher in elektronischer und gedruckter Form bringen das Fachwissen von Springerautor*innen kompakt zur Darstellung. Sie sind besonders für die Nutzung als eBook auf Tablet-PCs, eBook-Readern und Smartphones geeignet. *essentials* sind Wissensbausteine aus den Wirtschafts-, Sozial- und Geisteswissenschaften, aus Technik und Naturwissenschaften sowie aus Medizin, Psychologie und Gesundheitsberufen. Von renommierten Autor*innen aller Springer-Verlagsmarken.

Michael Treier

Corporate Health Management 4.0 in the Digital Age

 Springer

Michael Treier
Hochschule für Polizei und öffentliche Verwaltung NRW
Duisburg, Germany

ISSN 2197-6708   ISSN 2197-6716   (electronic)
essentials
ISBN 978-3-658-39336-6   ISBN 978-3-658-39337-3   (eBook)
https://doi.org/10.1007/978-3-658-39337-3

This Springer imprint is published by the registered company Springer Fachmedien Wiesbaden GmbH, part of Springer Nature.
The registered company address is: Abraham-Lincoln-Str. 46, 65189 Wiesbaden, Germany

What You Can Find in This *Essential*

- Arguments for a digital transformation strategy of the classic CHM to CHM 4.0
- Answers to the challenges of the working world 4.0 with regard to the modernization of CHM
- Guideposts for the conceptualization of a CHM 4.0 to avoid a digital odyssey during implementation
- Modular framework based on the building block principle for a digital corporate health model
- Presentation of relevant attributes of a digital toolbox
- Success factors and quality criteria in relation to CHM 4.0

This publication deliberately refrains from naming concrete digital tools ranging from apps to platforms from (non-)commercial manufacturers.

Contents

List of Abbreviations

BDSG	Federal Data Protection Act
CHM	Corporate Health Management (in German BGM)
D-CHM	Digital Occupational Health Management
DVG	Digital Supply Act
EAP	Employee Assistance Program
OHS	Occupational Health and Safety (in German AGS)
OIM	Operational Integration Management (in German BEM)
PDSG	Patient Data Protection Act
SGB	Social Security Code Book (Code of Social Law)
WHP	Workplace Health Promotion (in German BGF)

The digital impulse is unstoppable and is being taken up in the health sector by many actors in society and economy. Almost everyone in the workforce uses digital technologies. Digital concepts are infiltrating all domains of life. This is not hype, but reality. Corporate health management (CHM) can actively leverage this trend to increase its own relevance, penetration and sustainability. *"Apps and buttons"* can contribute to a healthy organization if the digital transformation in CHM is consistently implemented with regard to prevention and health promotion. New health risks such as digital stress must be taken into account.

An expert survey on the **future of corporate health management** makes it clear that digital tools in CHM meet with a positive response (Käfer and Niederberger 2019). This is underlined by the requirements of Work 4.0 (Sect. 1.2), the trend towards individualized health concepts (Sect. 1.3) and the priority given to digitalization (Sect. 1.4). In particular, a **digital offensive** is to be expected in the approaches of workplace health promotion (WHP) with regard to exercise, nutrition, recreation and stress management. Disease prevention (interventions that prevent the onset or spread of a disease) and health promotion (interventions that contribute to a healthy lifestyle) must be taken into account in equal measure in the digital model in order to achieve individual and collective **health gains** by reducing risk factors at the personal, technical and organisational level and strengthening protective factors and resources (Uhle and Treier 2019).

© The Author(s), under exclusive license to Springer Fachmedien   1
Wiesbaden GmbH, part of Springer Nature 2023
M. Treier, *Corporate Health Management 4.0 in the Digital Age*, essentials,
https://doi.org/10.1007/978-3-658-39337-3_1

1.1   The Digital Dam Burst as a Challenge

> The Corona pandemic has accelerated the digitalization push – some see this as a digital dam burst, others as a digital bubble. Health issues must not be sidelined in the digital age, while digitalization is in the fast lane.

Indicators on the **foundation of e-health** in society and economy such as *Digital Health Index of the Bertelsmann Foundation* or *eHealth Monitor of McKinsey & Company* confirm the turbulent development as fast track. The disruptive upheavals determine the digital concept as a **present model** to maintain the ability to act in healthcare (Haring 2019). But traditional CHM often does not show sufficient connectivity to digital concepts. Despite their popularity and the "Always on" way of life, digital models should not be hastily implemented in CHM.

Everything that can be digitized is in fact digitized, and after digitization comes virtualization (cf. D21 Digital Index, https://initiatived21.de). In a figurative sense, an analogous problem crystallises here as with Moore's law of information technology, which postulates an exponential development of IT performance, but this is limited by scientific laws. The question is not *whether* the digital transformation will lead to CHM 4.0, but *how* this transformation can be carried out successfully and in a quality-oriented manner while respecting these limits. The following **key questions** accompany this change.

- Do we need a transformation of CHM in the direction of digitalization?
- Which digital solutions are target-oriented for CHM?
- What potentials result from regulations such as the e-health law for apps & co.?
- How can digital health solutions be implemented in classic CHM?
- What trends in digital solutions can be expected in the future?

Potentials and risks reveal the **ambiguity** in dealing with the digital model with regard to healthy organization (Chap. 5) (Albrecht 2016; Matusiewicz and Kaiser 2018).

Positive effects can be found both on the employer side (e.g. employer image, cost reduction) and on the employee side (e.g. personalized offers, use in decentralized workplaces). **Critical aspects** relate not only to questions of data protection, but also to the unmanageable healthcare market, which makes a quality-oriented selection of digital healthcare tools difficult. Evidence on the effectiveness of the tools is often lacking.

In addition, there is a kind of **counter-movement** to digitalization in the health sector – the digital detox and the risk of self-measurement (self-hacking, lifelogging) are pointedly being discussed (Otto 2016; Selke 2016). The psychological and social implications of technologized self-observation have not yet been fully explored (Kalch and Wagner 2020). Health and fitness-related media content distributed across social media such as Instagram can impact mental health and body satisfaction and disrupt health socialization. The range of potential, i.e. positive as well as negative, media effects cannot be ignored from a health science perspective. However, in view of the trends, these findings will not lead to *"disconnect"*, but to a reflected *"reconnect"*, because the **digital umbilical cord** in lifestyle can no longer be separated. Certainly digital is not everything. Quality of life requires personal contact, but the digital model will change or even overturn this analogue approach.

Therefore, a successively **evaluated digital transformation of the health management system** is recommended rather than the rapid acquisition of health gadgets. In many cases, there is also a lack of media competence on the part of the user to make a smooth transition from the analog to the digital model. Accordingly, providers promise themselves a constructive approach to **digital normality in healthcare** from *blended corporate health* as a combination of analogue and digital tools, so that the user can gradually get used to the digital model. However, there is a risk here that digital approaches will only be taken into account in a complementary, but not autonomous way. As a result, the potential of the digital model is not explored, and the answers to the challenges of Work 4.0 may be too moderate.

1.2 Digital Health Concept as a Response to Work 4.0

CHM 4.0 is more than a portfolio of digital tools. Quality assurance, networking, control and administration are crucial in order to establish itself as a contemporary counterpart to Work 4.0. In this context, an artificial separation between the pillars of occupational health and safety and workplace health promotion is not expedient, as behavioral and environmental prevention concerning working conditions are inextricably interwoven in the digital world of work.

It is a truism that **health and Work 4.0** are intertwined. The "new world of work" (New Work) has a variety of positive and negative health effects (Fig. 1.1) (Social Health@Work 2020). **Research programs** such as *"Measures and*

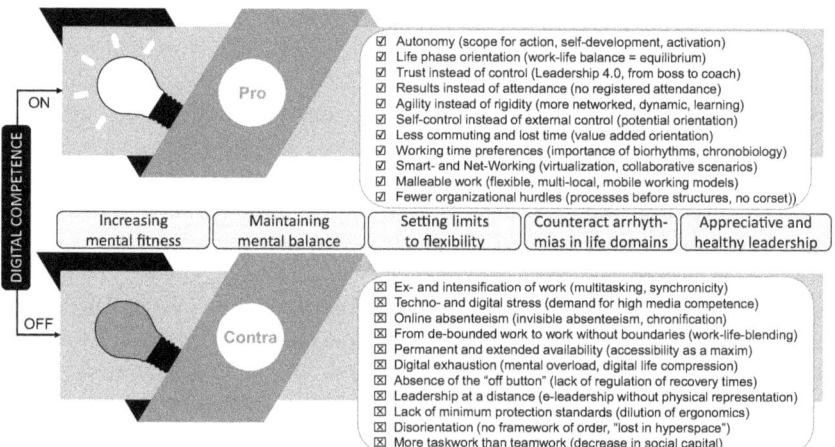

DIGITAL COMPETENCE

ON

Pro

☑ Autonomy (scope for action, self-development, activation)
☑ Life phase orientation (work-life balance = equilibrium)
☑ Trust instead of control (Leadership 4.0, from boss to coach)
☑ Results instead of attendance (no registered attendance)
☑ Agility instead of rigidity (more networked, dynamic, learning)
☑ Self-control instead of external control (potential orientation)
☑ Less commuting and lost time (value added orientation)
☑ Working time preferences (importance of biorhythms, chronobiology)
☑ Smart- and Net-Working (virtualization, collaborative scenarios)
☑ Malleable work (flexible, multi-local, mobile working models)
☑ Fewer organizational hurdles (processes before structures, no corset))

| Increasing mental fitness | Maintaining mental balance | Setting limits to flexibility | Counteract arrhythmias in life domains | Appreciative and healthy leadership |

OFF

Contra

☒ Ex- and intensification of work (multitasking, synchronicity)
☒ Techno- and digital stress (demand for high media competence)
☒ Online absenteeism (invisible absenteeism, chronification)
☒ From de-bounded work to work without boundaries (work-life-blending)
☒ Permanent and extended availability (accessibility as a maxim)
☒ Digital exhaustion (mental overload, digital life compression)
☒ Absence of the "off button" (lack of regulation of recovery times)
☒ Leadership at a distance (e-leadership without physical representation)
☒ Lack of minimum protection standards (dilution of ergonomics)
☒ Disorientation (no framework of order, "lost in hyperspace")
☒ More taskwork than teamwork (decrease in social capital)

Fig. 1.1 Implications of Work 4.0 from a health perspective

Recommendations for the Healthy Work of Tomorrow" reveal how CHM 4.0 is developing into a sustainable occupational health and safety (OHS) with the help of smart technologies and concepts (MEgA project, https://gesundearbeit-mega. de/). **Digital stress** in the world of work is a prominent topic (DGB 2016). Especially fluid and agile working environments require a positive stress mindset as a resilience factor. Research is being conducted into the health effects of new technologies (techno-stress). One keyword here is, for example, constant accessibility as a form of psychological stress (Treier 2020a). People must learn to deal with technologies in a healthy way, and organizations must learn to actively shape Work 4.0 (Werther and Bruckner 2018). And CHM has to think about prevention 4.0 in order not to stay behind the trends (Cernavin et al. 2018). However, Work 4.0 means more than just digitalization – this manifests itself in attributes such as agility, flexibility and adaptivity – the world of work is redefining itself (Hackl et al. 2017). Organizations are changing – becoming more learning and agile as the environment as a **VUCA world** becomes more *v*olatile, *u*ncertain, *c*omplex and *am*biguous. This has implications for the healthy organization and for everyone working there. It becomes critical when work and health drift apart.

The increasing flexibilization of working time and place of work in conjunction with the digitalization of the world of work is leading to new types of tasks and conditions (New Work), some of which are accompanied by extended autonomy. These trends are summarised as Work 4.0. The working world is becoming more agile and demands more competence from the employee in the area of self-regulation. Cloud working, desk sharing or mobile offices are characteristic of the fluid future model of work ("liquid workforce"), in which the boundaries between the working and private worlds are blurring. This blurring of boundaries entails new risks and demands high levels of resilience or psychological resistance from employees. (Uhle and Treier 2019, p. 607) (German quote translated by the author Treier)

4.0 processes determine all domains of life. Time and performance pressure are increasing, the density of communication and interaction is growing, psychological stress is rampant, multitasking and acceleration make it more difficult to regulate attention. 4.0 processes are to be determined as both a stress and strain factor. Intensification (quantitative and qualitative work density), more responsibility (job decision latitude or room for manoeuvre), hyper-flexibilization of working time and place of work, increased social physical isolation, more pronounced stress fluctuations, constant accessibility, dissolution of boundaries in work, increased demand for mobility are **attributes of Work 4.0.** CHM must accordingly make its offers more *flexible, modularized and personalized.* In addition, contents such as self-care and the ability to recover must be integrated into the portfolio.

> **CHM 4.0** is defined as a corporate health management adapted to the framework conditions of Work 4.0. A digital strategy enables the necessary networking and adaptivity to create connectivity to Work 4.0. The use of digital tools is taken up by D-CHM. CHM 4.0 is an expression of a modern occupational health strategy in the digital age.

The decisive effect of Work 4.0 is an **arrhythmia of lifetime,** because chronobiology is not only disturbed during shift work. Therefore, **Work 5.0** claims a healthy relationship between work and leisure (Ramb and Zaboroswki 2018). Leisure is not the time free from work, but the time that one claims for oneself personally. This is where CHM 4.0 can support to maintain the **digital balance.** CHM 4.0 thus expands from prevention management to **rhythm-of-life management.**

The answer to Work 4.0 is not to wait, but to activate. This takes place as **digital push** (CHM as a service) and **digital pull** (user expectations). On the one hand, it is necessary to motivate target groups to use digital health offers (push), on the other hand, health-conscious people actively search for corresponding offers in a healthy organization (pull). The impetus for digital health is often not provided by health institutions, but by the employees themselves.

For an effective digital strategy, it is important in the first phase to explore **the space of possibilities of digitalization,** taking into account the challenges of the agile working world, and to develop an integration concept with regard to voluntary and legally prescribed offers in CHM. This raises the question of what implications the digital health model has for **resources, processes and structures of CHM 4.0,** taking into account regulatory requirements such as the E-Health Act (Act on Secure Digital Communication and Applications in Healthcare).

> **Digital workplace health promotion (WHP) is not digital corporate health management (CHM),** because that would fall short and focus one-sidedly on health behaviour and personal responsibility. Nevertheless, it is advisable to start with WHP, because it is visible, tangible and effective. In this way, the digital impulse can gradually spread to other areas of the occupational health and safety through WHP as a pioneer. The CHM as an organizational concept remains, but its control and administration is realized as a virtual health center, in order to network actors in CHM and to link online and offline measures as *blended corporate health management* (Sect. 3.3).

The **e-health offers** in health promotion are tangible in the digital concept. They are implemented, for example, as fitness apps in the area of exercise or nutrition coaching. According to the #whatsnext2020 study (IFBG 2020, p. 60), digital health promotion is already a reality in 13.5% of organisations and a further 14% are in the planning stage. However, CHM 4.0 is not limited to the application of digital offerings. This would not exhaust the potential. Rather, systematic networking and management of the digital and analogue health worlds within the framework of **holistic health management** is required in order to adequately integrate digital offerings into the **prevention matrix of the healthy organization** and to increase their effectiveness through synergy effects (Chap. 3). Furthermore, not only the popular approach of behavioral prevention, but also that of environmental prevention concerning working conditions must be taken into account (Sect. 4.3).

> **The Question is Not Whether You Want to Start Digital, But Just How**
> Despite the conflicting empirical evidence on the effectiveness and benefits of digital health offerings, the 4.0 trend in health promotion as a response to the attributes of Work 4.0 can no longer be stopped. But a digital model that only uses digital and mobile formats in workplace health promotion or enriches the latter with digital offerings is not CHM 4.0, because the decisive factor here is that the healthy organization links analog and digital approaches in prevention management, controls them and evaluates them with regard to their effectiveness. What is needed here is a management system for safety and health at work.

1.3 Individualisation as a Megatrend

More responsibility for one's own health is the maxim of modern health promotion. § 1 of the German Social (Security) Code Book V (SGB V) underlines this, as those affected are expected to lead a health-conscious lifestyle, to take precautions at an early stage and to play an active role in prevention and therapy. Irrespective of the question of how much self-responsibility can be expected of people, the requirement remains that health and prevention services should be geared to the individual. The latter requires a personalization of the company health strategy.

Digital trends such as the *Quantified Self Movement* focus on self-monitoring and self-management with regard to a health-promoting lifestyle. For example, digital self-measurement in fitness is an ongoing trend. This is more than hype, this represents a **transformative force.** The Techniker Krankenkasse (German health insurance company) speaks here of **Homo Digivitalis** (TK 2018). Increasingly, digital tools are used that take into account the participants' peculiarities and demands as *Personalized Health* (Käfer and Niederberger 2019). The **risks of digital self-measurement** lie in the area of surveillance and discrimination, especially when institutions such as insurance companies, employers or banks are involved. Health psychologists are also critically concerned with the connections between health and personal responsibility (Sect. 4.2), because the premise for an emancipated and healthy lifestyle is a well-developed **health literacy** (Schaeffer and Pelikan 2017).

The future goal is a **wearable and everyday health promotion** through smart interfaces that are close to the body and a prevention work that is independent of location and time, is individually designed and flexible, enables analyses and provides feedback, sets activation impulses and proves to be suitable for use (usability). The distinction between medicine, health and wellness is fluid. Health literacy education is deinstitutionalized, modularized and personalized. Collaborative learning settings enable social exchange in networks. Prerequisites are an appropriate **level of digital maturity of the health tools** and a **high level of self-regulation competence** among users in the sense of digital readiness.

Self-determined, self-effective and responsible, but not overconfident health consumers are necessary so that personalized health offers can effectively contribute to a healthy lifestyle. Many employees already use health apps on their smartphones, wear wearables (e.g. fitness bracelets), sometimes smart clothes, or use self-checks on the Internet, as surveys by the digital association Bitkom show (https://www.bitkom.org/). There is hardly any **fear of contact** with *"gadgets and widgets"* in the areas of health, lifestyle and fitness. Almost 70–80% of Internet users access to "Dr. Google" et al. for information on health risks and behaviour. **Digital health** is asserting itself as a progressive trend, replacing the *one-size-fits-all principle* as a standard clothing size in favor of *tailored programs to* achieve higher compliance in prevention and motivation in health promotion.

However, the empirical evidence also shows the **dark side,** because the explosive growth of the digital health market harbours risks that not only concern the "datacracy" in the health sector as the instrumentalization of **sensitive health data**. There is also the danger of a **digital odyssey**, as there are hardly any guidelines for systematic implementation. The crucial issue concerns the question of appropriate content. In the area of prevention work, for example, **fake news** can make persuasion and selection of offers more difficult, because many people may believe that they have good **health literacy** due to the digital availability and comprehensibility of health information. However, this *health literacy* is by no means as high in Germany, as it is shown that more than half have limited health literacy (Schaeffer et al. 2017). There is often a significant discrepancy between health awareness and action, as nutrition reports from the German Nutrition Society (www.dge.de) or the Federal Health Surveys reveal (www.degs-studie.de). For example, if 61% of respondents believe that their health status is good, but only 9% really live healthily (DKV 2018), then this contradiction cannot be solved by digitalization, but only by **health literacy management** (Uhle and Treier 2019). Figure 1.2 illustrates the challenges in CHM 4.0 based on the results of the study on digital health literacy (TK 2018).

> **Digital health literacy** means that information and communication technologies are used confidently, purposefully and self-critically by individuals to maintain, promote or restore their health.

Health 4.0 represents a paradigm shift: The role of the participant is no longer to be defined *as a patient,* but *as a customer.* Health becomes a product. Regulation is decreasing. Wellness, prevention, diagnostics and therapy become

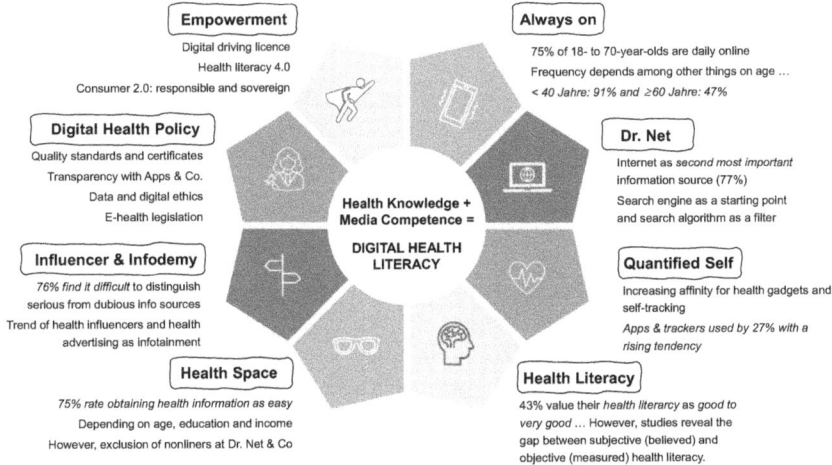

Fig. 1.2 Digital health literacy based on TK (2018)

blurred, because the employee is no longer black and white healthy or sick. Healthy, acutely and chronically ill people as well as occupationally rehabilitated persons form the heterogeneous target group in CHM. Health apps, wearables and health centers make it possible to tailor health promotion to the needs of each employee. This can be implemented regardless of whether employees are located in a company headquarters or branch office and regardless of when employees want to be active, whether before, during or after work. This makes CHM 4.0 **independent of time and place** and opens up new perspectives for companies and employees. To achieve this, the offers must adapt to the varying contexts, which is realized by mobile health approaches (Sect. 4.1).

> **The CHM of the Modern Age is Not a CHM of the Masses**
> Deregulation, decentralization and deinstitutionalization are the prerequisites for tailor-made CHM. The individual develops a personal health concept in a self-determined manner with experts in CHM. Technically, personalization can be implemented, but the challenge remains to promote health and media competence of the users in addition to self-regulation as an empowerment strategy.

1.4   Drivers of CHM 4.0

> No one will deny the powerful digital impulses. They come from all spheres, i.e. business, society, education, jurisprudence or technology. Digital pressure is inevitable. For too long, CHM has resisted consistent digitalization and is in danger of losing its ability to connect to the digital age.

Global megatrends such as demographic change, globalization, individualization and the knowledge society are leaving their mark on CHM (Matusiewicz and Kaiser 2018). Figure 1.3 illustrates primary and secondary **drivers of digitalization** (Bertelsmann 2016). If CHM does not want to lose touch with the digital world and the working world of tomorrow (New Work), then CHM must transform into CHM 4.0. Ubiquitous are streaming services, video chats from sports lessons to conferences to webinars, online platforms, Internet of Things, e-commerce – a digital encounter is pre-programmed. **Digitalization in the healthcare sector** in particular is gaining considerable momentum (Sect. 4.1). In the healthcare market, you will not only find health apps and wearables as scalable mass products, but also personalized instruments such as online coaching and EAP (neutral advice for employees) up to digital CHM/OIM complete systems. This technological zenith is

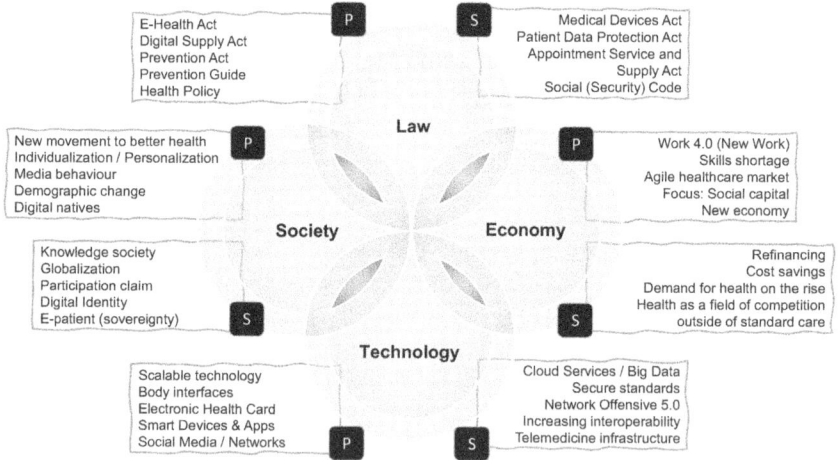

Fig. 1.3 Primary and secondary drivers related to CHM 4.0

accompanied by a **cultural change,** because users see themselves as sovereign, proactive and emancipated in contrast to the image of the passive and enduring patient in healthcare.

Apps on prescription, digital helpers for migraine, insomnia, lack of exercise, stress, digestive problems, anxiety management to digitally assisted tooth brushing – there are no limits. The health market is exploding, and jurisdiction is reacting. **Legal impulses for digitalization** are provided by the E-Health Act, Prevention Act 2015, SGB V/IX, the DVG (Digital Supply Act) and PDSG (Patient Data Protection Act) (Krüger-Brand 2019). CHM 4.0 can benefit from current legislation, for example in the refinancing of digital services by social insurance providers. Nevertheless, technical innovations are often groundbreaking, but legal regulations remain behind.

This pressure to digitize also comes up against a **digital working world** (Sect. 1.1), which not only provides the technical infrastructure, but also manifests a positive attitude among employees with regard to the digital transformation as a *digital mindset.* The critical arguments of data protection with regard to digitalization in CHM can be put into perspective to some extent, because new technologies and authentication channels enable **higher security standards** (Sect. 3), such as *blockchain* as tamper-proof storage of data in linked data blocks. Whether it will even go so far in the future that, for example, a digital twin (virtual patient) will be used in medicine to test personalized therapies can only be guessed at present, but it does reveal the scope for digitization with the aid of blockchain technology (Million 2019, p. 89ff.).

In addition, **media behaviour** has changed drastically in recent years, so that defensive reactions to digital health and prevention offers are diminishing. Even the Corona pandemic crisis manifests how adaptable employees are. What previously seemed only manageable in analog or offline mode can now be accomplished in online mode. Nevertheless, it should be noted that the majority of users are not *digital natives,* if only because of their age structure. Presumably, however, the digital natives are a driving force for the comprehensive mapping of the D-CHM.

Another driver is **cost savings** in accordance with § 2 of the German Social (Security) Code Book V (SGB V), which requires compliance with the principle of economic efficiency. This also affects the CHM. To realize more offers without quality losses requires a D-CHM. Online prevention courses can be tax-exempt according to § 3.34 Income Tax Act. Funding by health insurance companies is conceivable if online offers are certified (GKV 2020; ZPP 2020). Various formats from online courses and webinars to health coaching and health serious games are eligible for funding. Communities, forums and information platforms are excluded.

Drivers promise **high penetration of digital tools**. Is this promise or reality? Our own health surveys on the question *"Do you already successfully use digital tools such as wearables, fitness coaches or health apps in everyday life?"* still tend to document a reserved result, with only just under 16% clearly affirming this and around 15% stating "now and then" (N = 1021, employees of different organizations). The result indicates that there is still room for improvement in the digital agenda in the workplace health promotion.

Digital Health Agenda
The political statement is a mantra: *We must not lose touch!* The prerequisites are being created from a technical, political, economic and legal perspective, but CHM often lags behind innovation and looks back too often. Don't be afraid of digitalization in CHM is the motto, because it is unstoppable and infiltrates all domains of life.

Fields of Action in CHM 4.0

2

The future of CHM is digitalized, personalized and networked. CHM 4.0 creates an integrated platform to equally understand the claim of organizational and individual fitness as a win-win situation. The base is a healthy organization. The digital model links environmental prevention concerning working conditions and behavioural prevention. Low-threshold personalized access to information, communication and transaction as fields of action of CHM act as door openers to a healthy organization.

The digital linking of behavioural prevention and environmental prevention concerning working conditions characterizes a holistic prevention model as a virtual health centre (Chap. 3). From the point of view of content, the digital model is built on three pillars in order to cluster the diverse range of services in health management (Fig. 2.1). **The portfolio of digital corporate health management (D-CHM)** ranges from fitness trackers to information systems and health software up to online coaching. Smartphones, tablets and wearables enable health behaviour independent of time and place (mobile health). They thus take into account the de facto dissolution of the boundaries of life domains. **Digital health** subsumes information, communication and transaction as fields of action.

Digital health is "the collaborative and/or interactive application of modern information and communication technologies to improve health care and population health." (Bertelsmann 2016, p. 7) (German quote translated by the author Treier)

© The Author(s), under exclusive license to Springer Fachmedien Wiesbaden GmbH, part of Springer Nature 2023
M. Treier, *Corporate Health Management 4.0 in the Digital Age*, essentials, https://doi.org/10.1007/978-3-658-39337-3_2

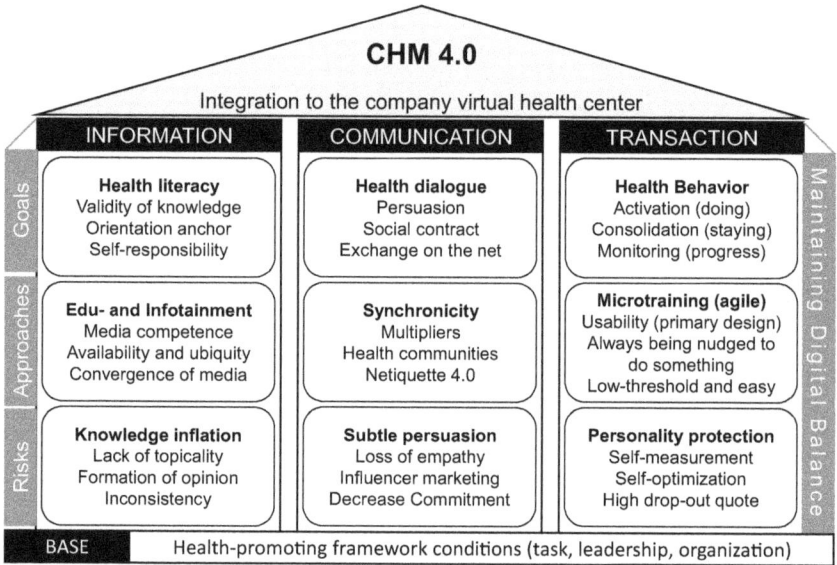

Fig. 2.1 Fields of action in CHM 4.0

2.1 Information in CHM 4.0

Valid knowledge in the health sector is a challenge. There is a wealth of knowledge about health, but users are often overwhelmed when it comes to finding their way through the jungle of health tips and separating the wheat from the chaff. Without the availability of up-to-date and valid health knowledge, however, the basis for healthy behavior in organizations is missing.

The **information pillar** is a fundamental building block in the digital health model and targets health literacy (Schaeffer and Pelikan 2017).

Health literacy is multidimensional. It enables people to shape their lives in a health-conscious way and to make use of health care services in a self-responsible and self-regulatory manner in order to lead a healthy lifestyle.

CHM 4.0 supports users in finding, understanding, evaluating and applying health information. In view of the hyperinflation of health media presentations and contradictory health recommendations, including fake news in the sense of **infodemics,** this is proving to be a difficult task. In our own health surveys, just under 39% state that they regularly inform themselves about health-related topics on the Internet, but only about 18% trust this information when it comes to their own health (N = 1435, employees from different organizations). From a health psychology perspective, the ability to self-direct is also fundamental so that knowledge does not result in inert knowledge but in **action-oriented health literacy** (Sect. 4.2) (Knoll et al. 2017).

Health knowledge exists, but the ability to master it in the digital age is often lacking. A **digital driver's license for health literacy** is needed (Langkafel and Matusiewicz 2021). Due to the uncontrolled and overflowing inflation of health information, **guidance** is needed that also helps to immunize against infodemics. Such filtered and edited information can be implemented on an organization's intranet. If an organization's own expertise is limited, it makes sense to refer to tested information platforms, such as the German platform www.psyga.info or the National Health Platform https://gesund.bund.de. The interdisciplinary project " *Orientation guide in dealing with digital health information offers* " (OriGes) takes a somewhat different approach. The website www.gesund-im-netz.net provides help for online research on health topics.

In order to counteract disorientation, *knowledge impulses* are to be set *as orientation anchors* without acting as influencers or testimonials (Sect. 2.2). It is primarily about **infotainment** in the sense of the T_3 concept, i.e. *"tips, tricks and tickers".* It is advisable to link to validated knowledge on the Internet and to provide assistance for online research. Whether one thinks about company wiki or blogs as an extension is mainly due to the availability of resources and in particular the personnel capacity to attend to the digital platform. With regard to linking, it should be noted that with "Dr. Internet" many advice sites, health portals and online encyclopaedias do not provide quality-assured information and that uncertainty and ambiguity are determining factors with regard to health topics. Following **psychoeducation**, it is important to make well-founded health knowledge accessible and understandable and to trigger concern in order to increase compliance to deal with one's health in a self-determined manner.

The **availability of information,** e.g. via portals, webinars, health podcasts, health forums and newsletters, is elementary in order to raise awareness and provide orientation. However, it should be noted that in the working world, attention spans are relatively short, so that health knowledge competes for attention and can only claim it for fleeting periods. Since users access the organization's health information in different ways, responsive and adaptive design is required to make the **information available regardless of location or time** due to the variability of end-user devices. The display quality and logic of the user interface must be standardized according to software ergonomic quality criteria in accordance with ISO 9241.

> **Accessibility, Ease and Convenience of Health Information**
> The decisive factor is not the amount of valid information, but the offer of comprehensible orientation anchors as stimulus for own independent and qualified information research. Health marketing can promote explorative behaviour.

2.2   Communication in CHM 4.0

> In the age of Web 2.0, asynchronous and synchronous formats are converging in exchange. Networking enables more synchronicity in corporate health management. From a communication point of view, home office and remote concepts have become indispensable in occupational health strategies in order to reach employees regardless of location and time and to promote interaction.

More health through communication is the credo in the digital age. Wikis, micro- and weblogs such as Twitter, social networks such as Facebook, information and assessment portals, and sharing portals such as Instagram characterize **interpersonal and mass-media communication formats** in the digital health age (digital social sharing) (Altendorfer 2017; Kalch and Wagner (2020). The boundary between information, communication and marketing in the health sector is becoming increasingly blurred when, for example, podcasts become live podcasts or health-conscious people hardly manage to escape the hype of health influencers. The willingness to share personal data publicly and digitally (running apps) is steadily increasing through to the use of a digital health record (personal health recording, self- and public tracking) (Sect. 3.1). The merging of different information and communication channels in the sense of a **digital convergence of health media** creates potential, but also risks in the area of data and privacy protection. *Can these effects of social media use in health care be classified as positive or do* *they negatively influence self-critical health education?* These and other questions affect the field of communication (Hurrelmann and Baumann 2014). *Can this trend be used constructively in CHM 4.0 or should CHM 4.0 consciously distance itself from it?*

In the health sector, a distinction is made between **bloggers** (authors on the web, varying formats from experience reports to journalism to science blogs), **influencers** (storytelling via Instagram & Co, from mega- to micro-influencers, from professionals to those affected) and **testimonials** (advocates for health products or messages). In view of the need for exchange and hunger for information on health topics, the roles are visibly shifting into one another – what they have in common is that protagonists provide orientation on the web. It is often difficult for followers or researchers to recognize whether this is a format of subtle marketing (persuasion) or authentic enlightenment beyond classic media. A look at sources or references, education and background of the person as well as the occurrence of advertising can reveal how serious the communication channel is.

Due to its inherent dynamics, a communication concept is more difficult to implement than the implementation of an editorially prepared information platform. However, CHM 4.0 does not only want to inform, but also to participate and give space to social interactions. The migration between private and company social networks is particularly difficult. Therefore, it is fundamental for the communication field that **guidelines** for communication exist in order to ensure respectful, moral and factually appropriate interaction as netiquette. Particularly for the sensitive area of health, there is a need for a **social media strategy** with transparent communication guidelines that refer back to an **ethics of digitalization** within the framework of a digital policy (Schnell in Scherenberg and Pundt 2018, p. 277ff.). The depth of communication in CHM 4.0 varies from health blogs and support forums to chats and online coaching to virtual health or prevention teams. The same rules apply to all these formats.

According to Altendorfer (2017, p. 34 f.), communication as a field of action is not only about the consumption of health information, but also about active influence, social motivation, exchange of interests and knowledge, and behavioural change. Many of these communicative processes take place autonomously and are not moderated – **health communities** with a lifestyle orientation are created. Thus, a company running club can use social networks for administration, but also for exchange (storytelling) and motivation, as well as setting competitive impulses (challenges) and increasing the reach of followers.

Here, CHM 4.0 provides a **communication platform** with a code of conduct. The accompanying e-coaching is important as a **response and interaction model** (Sect. 3.3). Similar to the EAP, internal or external health coaching can promote the (mental) health and performance of employees in a timely manner, especially in critical situations – here, communication becomes transaction (Sect. 2.3). Synchronous communication formats dominate, which are classically analogue, but also take place by telephone, chat room or video conference. This **interpersonal communication** is only the tip of the iceberg. For many topics can also be worked out in autonomous or moderated self-help groups or in virtual health teams. Here, despite decentralized organization, the digital format allows people with similar challenges and expectations to be linked. Care must be taken to avoid subtle marketing with persuasive influence creeping into the social network. An online reporting system can counter this risk.

It is clear that **CHM** enters into **dialogue** (Uhle and Treier 2019, p. 238ff.). *Do good and talk about it!* Digital formats enable location- and time-independent communication and linking of people who have no social ties. The transition between health information campaigns (health campaigning) and health advice as a transaction (health counselling or consulting) is often fluid and not clearly defined. Partner, ambassador or pilot are roles that make it clear that the **multiplier approach** dominates in the field of communication in order to pass on and disseminate health knowledge through dialogue. The participants themselves become instructors.

However, experts in health communication fear that the **authenticity of the dialogue** can be lost through digitalization. *Will the health message be de-emotionalized through digitalization?* **Emotions** are important in the health sector when it comes to living and experiencing. Missionary information (cognition) – live healthy – often remains ineffective if it is not emotionally based. In the field of communication, the information as perception (Sect. 2.1), which is predominantly oriented towards cognition, must be enriched by affective moments accompanying interaction in dialogue formats in order to achieve an **activating reception of information.** Social exchange – e.g. between employees and health coordinators – creates new social contexts and enables **digital empathy.** Research is being conducted in this area, especially in the field of digital patient communication (Kalch and Wagner 2020). The challenge is therefore to create a **digital balance in terms of information and emotion** and to act as a link between the *authentically emotional and the receptive digital health world.* Health topics can be communicated with humor, internal health representatives drive the topic forward with personality. The motto is: *"Health moves"*, whether in digital or analogue mode.

Expanded, it is then no longer just about digital exchange processes and their facilitation, but about a **culture of health and trust,** when it is no longer just about individuals and their range of interaction in the micro- and mesocosmos, but diverse stakeholders such as managers pull together on the rope of the healthy organization (Uhle and Treier 2019).

> **Communication as an Agile Moment in CHM 4.0**
> Diversity of communication channels, media convergence, use of synchronous formats and professional response management outline challenges in CHM 4.0. The field of communication is process-related and refers equally to health communication and health marketing. Some communication channels describe transactions, because communication can move and activate from a health perspective.

2.3   Transactions in CHM 4.0

> In the digital age, transactions are not only more diverse, but also more tailored and break new ground, for example in the field of augmented reality. However, this chapter is not about future scenarios, but about accessibility, reach and low-threshold as basic requirements. Health education takes place in stages, independent of time and place, in a microformat – this learning concept fundamentally determines the transactions, which are characterized by ease and convenience.

Section 4.1 introduces the digital toolbox as the nucleon of transactions. At this point, the focus is on **general design parameters.** Classic CHM focuses primarily on transactions that require a relatively high level of attention and time commitment. In CHM 4.0, there is a paradigm shift here towards **microlearning** or microtraining (training in small bites) in order to integrate the methods into everyday working life in a way that conserves resources and thus enables health education close to the workplace (Burkhart & Hanser in Matusiewicz and Kaiser 2018, p. 51 f.). **Learning nuggets** (gold nuggets) as a short format benefit from the digital transformation. The size of the nuggets depends on content and didactics to ward off fragmented learning as a risk.

In **microlearning,** health education takes place in stages or in a short format in order to allow learning independent of time and place. This low-threshold transaction is suitable for consolidating (adherence) and internalizing (elaboration) what has been learned in everyday activities, as the learning units are not perceived as disruptive. Health education takes place en passant as incidential learning. These multimedia stimuli use videos, short breaks, playful elements or infographics. The underlying *learning nuggets* are designed in a varied way in order to ignite their motivational effect. From a didactic point of view, the learning nuggets can be linked to hierarchically structured learning objectives. Sequencing (chronological order) and segmentation (information units) of the learning material prevent mental overload in digital formats. Modular concepts enable the development of more comprehensive units of competence.

This paradigm shift does not imply pulling the analog plug. In **blended learning,** for example, analogue attendance slots can be combined with digital microformats for intensification. Health messages can be packaged in an entertaining way (edu- and infotainment) or suggestions for health behaviour can be conveyed non-invasively. In this way, **agile learning** is achieved with regard to health literacy. Agile learning here means self-organized, networked, digital and personalized. Profile-based networking with others is to be arranged with the help of social networks, so that **social learning** is also made possible. From a business perspective, these learning nuggets are cost-effective, scalable and adaptable to expectations. Furthermore, the development of the nuggets can be done by authoring tools without external help, if expertise in content mapping is available.

In the case of **self-development**, it should be noted that not only the content but also the didactic design are decisive for the success of microlearning (cf. Niegemann and Weinberger 2020). However, from a psychological and pedagogical perspective, the professionalization of instructional design often lags behind technological educational innovation.

Low-threshold and practical offers should not induce additional stress, but help to pursue health goals in the reality check of everyday working life (Fig. 2.2). For example, a micro-break could encourage people to do exercises to strengthen their neck muscles at their computer workstations, if the public traffic allows it.

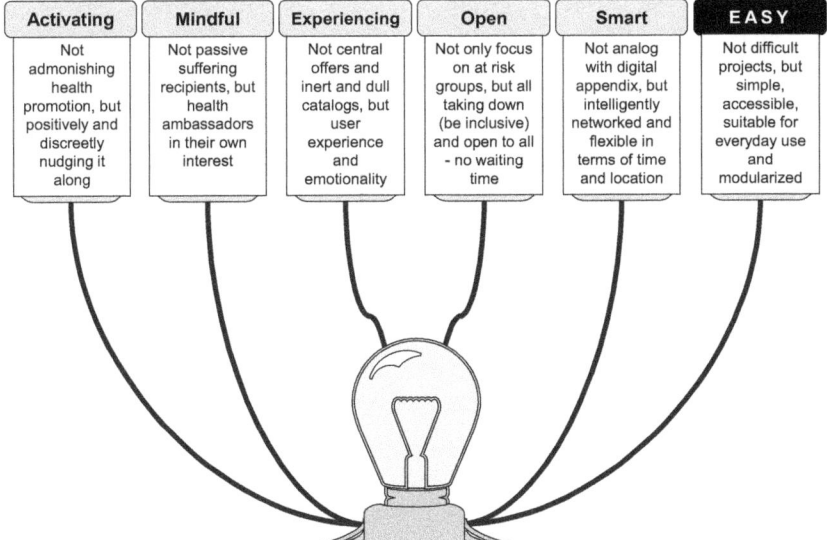

Activating	Mindful	Experiencing	Open	Smart	EASY
Not admonishing health promotion, but positively and discreetly nudging it along	Not passive suffering recipients, but health ambassadors in their own interest	Not central offers and inert and dull catalogs, but user experience and emotionality	Not only focus on at risk groups, but all taking down (be inclusive) and open to all - no waiting time	Not analog with digital appendix, but intelligently networked and flexible in terms of time and location	Not difficult projects, but simple, accessible, suitable for everyday use and modularized

Fig. 2.2 Discovering ease in the digital health model

Analogous to **nudging** in marketing as a behavioural economic approach, the addressee who is a consumer of health is respected as consumer 2.0 in the health sector (e-patient) (Rose in Matusiewicz et al. 2021, p. 163ff.). *Nudging* without pressure and admonition is the maxim of adult-oriented didactics. The users are sensitized by pulsed learning elements and thereby develop their own pull to deepen the topic in a self-organized way. Scoring, gamification and interactive modules increase this pull.

In addition to low-threshold and accessibility, **key attributes of transactions** in CHM 4.0 are usability, user experience, easy operability, barrier-free accessibility, and retrievability as required (on-demand). The full-time employee on site is a discontinued model. In the modern world of work, decentralized workplaces and flexible working time models are dominant. Therefore, CHM 4.0 must focus on **increasing the range** in terms of quantity, location and time, because otherwise there is a risk that addressees will be excluded. For example, employees working part-time and/or in mobile workplaces are less likely to participate in traditional health education measures. Despite the increased reach and easy accessibility, individuals still need to be "nudged" to get into the fairway of workplace health promotion. This is best done through a token system linked to digital media as an **incentive.** A positive response is achieved through a **health motivation model** that takes into account *intrinsic* (activation through content), *extrinsic* (activation through reward) and *social* (activation through others) motivators and is based on the health psychological construct of self-efficacy (Sect. 4.2) (Knoll et al. 2017).

Microformats as Gold Nuggets
Transactions in CHM 4.0 are low-threshold, easily accessible, intuitive to use, activating and can be integrated into everyday working life. They have a positive incentive-contribution ratio and thus create a high level of commitment. These microformats as *gold nuggets* are to be linked in a personalized learning plan and transparently mapped as a journal of transactions in order to meet the requirement of modularization. Incentive management supports the probability of participation and reduces drop-outs.

Integration as a Virtual Health Center

Programs in the fields of information, communication and transaction are not isolated interventions, but are to be linked as a prevention matrix. Personalization, monitoring and coordination are central features of the virtual health center to create order in the digital chaos.

Properly managed, the digital transformation and the increase in flexible work will make us healthier and more efficient. (Stephan Böhm, University of St. Gallen) (Social Health@Work 2020, p. 2) (German quote translated by the author Treier)

Information, communication and transaction are not to be understood as isolated approaches, but are combined as a holistic health model. A multidimensional prevention matrix is the basis for implementing a **multi-component programme** in corporate health management (CHM). In the digital prevention model, the starting points of behaviour and circumstances (prevention approaches) as well as the primary, secondary and tertiary stages are taken into account (Uhle and Treier 2019) (Fig. 3.1). Depending on the maturity level of CHM, three **integration levels** can be differentiated:

1. *Extension:* With the Adnex strategy, everything in CHM remains the same, but expanded with digital offerings – mostly at the information level (add-on). This rudimentary entry into the digital model can be implemented quickly, but is often not sustainable.

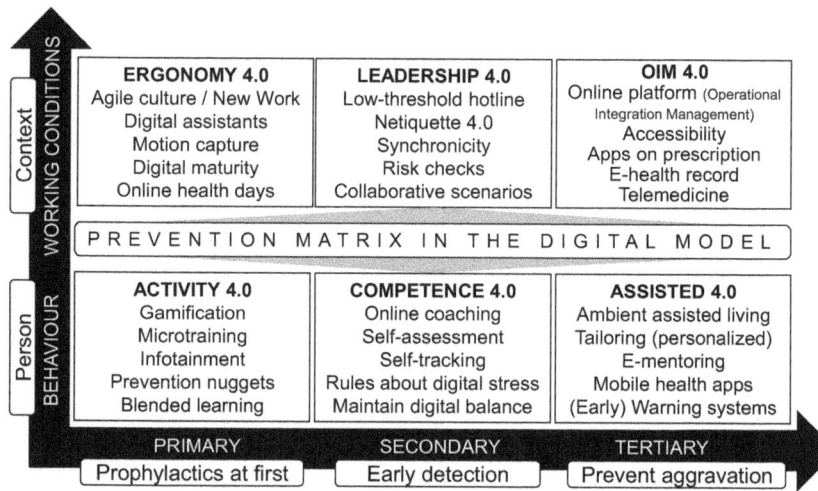

Fig. 3.1 Prevention matrix in CHM 4.0 – exemplary starting points

2. *Step by step:* In the substitution strategy, everything that can be meaningfully digitized from a content and didactic perspective is digitized step by step. The CHM as a control concept remains in the classic mode for the time being. In the workplace health promotion, the digital mode is focused on, and successively a transformation to D-CHM takes place.
3. *Blended:* In the transformation strategy, the digital model has the right of way in content, administration and management as a consistent and coherent path to the digital health model. Digital approaches are enriched by analogue offers and vice versa. The CHM transforms to CHM 4.0.

There is no simple *blueprint* for CHM 4.0. Maintaining order crystallizes as a challenge in the integration. The exploding variety of offers along with the demand for personalization require a **flexible framework** that takes the work-life balance into account. A **digital platform** serves as a starting point for administration and control. The project should be initiated by the CHM circle, represented by the works council, HR management, occupational medicine and occupational health and safety, among others. Concerted action promises to be more effective here. The PDCA cycle (Plan, Do, Check, Act) serves as a management model.

A fundamental question needs to be asked in advance: *Does it make sense to proceed with a limited pilot or across the board?* A prototype test has the advantage that the desire to explore is more likely to be given than in the case of an area-wide roll-out. On the other hand, the CHM 4.0 project is slowed down because several health models and different approaches coexist. A **limiting strategy** is nevertheless to be preferred due to many imponderables, but should not concern the scope, but rather the content focus. At the beginning, it is recommended to focus the content centres on **health communication and behavioural prevention,** as these dominate in the private living environment and cause less fear of contact among those involved (gateway model to achieve more acceptance). In addition, the market offers proven instruments here.

3.1   Health Current Account as a Personal Control Unit

"Health implies wealth" could be the maxim of an individual health record that provides information about the prevention process as a journal and acts as a basis for sustainable care. The health current account as a personal e-health record represents a personal control unit and is the key to the virtual health center.

In multi-level prevention programmes, participants and caregivers (e.g. advisors) need a diary (journal) of perceptions and progress in the management of personal health. The **health current account** can be implemented as an analogue or virtual card and has similarities to the digital patient record (Electronic Health Record). The analogue format requires a reader as hardware, but has the advantage that users have more confidence in the security of their data (card as data safe). In the form of a current account, prevention and health services can be administered in a self-determined manner and health credits and balances can be settled. The health current account is suitable for the participant-related recording of all health-related parameters and serves as a sustainable care instrument (Treier 2020b). It enables seamless **information management,** so that the specialist staff involved can provide effective support. *Data sovereignty is the exclusive responsibility of the owners.*

Concerns about privacy can be put into perspective if sufficient security precautions are taken from a technical point of view and the health current account is designed as a closed and transparent system. Verified data security facilitates acceptance – your system gets a seal of quality or approval according to TÜV (German association for technical inspection). It should be mentioned that self-measurement in media use (e.g. fitness apps) is already part of everyday routine for many people. Numerous users store and process personal, vital and health data in health apps on their smartphone, PC or console. There are also more and more health portals that accompany individual health management. In terms of self-determination its crucial, how the personal data is used and whether the collection achieves an individual benefit (Rosset et al. in Kalch and Wagner 2020, p. 117ff.). Transparent communication and access can reduce the **intention barrier** to the recording of data in a health current account.

> The availability of personal data is subject to input and transmission by the employee in the sense of **informational self-determination** (data ownership). From a legal point of view, the Federal Data Protection Act, the Freedom of Information Act, EU data protection directives and the EU General Data Protection Regulation (GDPR, in German DSGVO) must be taken into account. Transparent and data-protected implementation ensures privacy and data protection. The *right to informational privacy* means comprehensive control over collection, use and dissemination of personal health information analogous to the ID card in Estonia as the backbone of the digital society (https://e-estonia.com/solutions/e-identity/id-card/). Technology acceptance can only be achieved through self-determination.

The health current account acts as a **central key for the virtual health centre,** which not only documents and archives the course of interventions, but also stores interests and settings for personalizing the health centre (Sect. 3.3). The key creates a unified and **secure access system** to services, eliminating the need for changing access points. A synchronisation of various applications with existing interoperability takes place via the health current account. Basic functions are, for example, an electronic health calendar, self-assessment or an individually configured health alarm clock. The database-based mapping also enables connection to a token system as a points system for the purpose of incentivization (incentive management).

The health current account represents the digital tool for **managing one's own health.** Only the owners and supervisors or advisers approved by the owner have access to the data. Exclusively the owners decide on the release of data, for example in connection with coaching or evaluation processes in organizations. In addition, the level of detail and anonymity of the information can be defined.

The Path to Electronic Health Identity
An electronic identity in the healthcare sector can no longer be stopped and is necessary in view of the complex healthcare system and the dissolution of the boundaries between the spheres of life. A "frightened" and possibly paralyzing data protection must be taken into account in the planning and implementation of CHM 4.0, because data security crystallizes as a hardly forgiving basic claim in case of violation.

3.2   IT-Based Health Monitoring for Quality Assurance

IT-based health monitoring identifies risks (prevention), determines successes (legitimacy) and increases effectiveness (sustainability). Health monitoring is the backbone of the healthy organization and thus a core instrument of the virtual health center.

Healthy organisations need a digital **pilot and navigation system** to preserve and promote fragile human and social capital in the choppy waters of Working World 4.0 (Treier 2020b). Health controlling relies on asynchronous survey instruments, e.g. health surveys, risk assessment of mental stress or absenteeism analysis (Uhle and Treier 2019). Here, CHM 4.0 is undergoing a **change from output controlling to activity-oriented monitoring** as a formative evaluation.

Health controlling records pecuniary and structural aspects in accordance with the health strategy. From an operational point of view, it is a summative evaluation that takes place ex post and serves to compare strategic goals. **Health monitoring** focuses on process-related and content-related aspects in order to draw conclusions about events and effects of ongoing health processes in the sense of formative evaluation. Here, input and impact indicators are taken into account in particular. The **evaluation set of the healthy organization** links health monitoring and controlling in order to prepare decision-relevant information as **health reporting**.

The design of the **evaluation set** takes into account needs analysis (initial analysis on expectations and conditions), process (implementation), success (outcome measurement) and transfer controlling (effectiveness measurement). From the perspective of D-CHM, **micro-modules** are particularly relevant in order to enable accompanying monitoring of health activities. **Micro-monitoring** is non-invasive, designed to be low-threshold (e.g. prompts as short queries on health behaviour), can provide feedback and is integrated as an element in the health intervention. The screening is less oriented towards success factors of individual health (e.g. weight reduction) but is conative (indicators of activity level) according to the motto that effort is more important than outcome. CHM 4.0 pursues the primary goal that participants take advantage of the offers and translate them into their everyday work.

The virtual health center needs this information, on the one hand, to provide feedback to the participants and, on the other hand, to elicit organizational health values from an evaluation perspective on the basis of anonymized data. CHM can thus justify expenditures or investments in health measures at the organizational level. In order to avoid media discontinuities and to ensure that information management functions smoothly, **digital approaches** such as online-supported surveys, mobile and event-related recording of health-relevant data, anonymized participation and retention figures, activity rates for health measures, sensors at the workplace and at home (e.g. sitting time, posture recognition at the workplace) are promising.

- **Primary Use:** Monitoring is used to reinforce positive health behaviors. For example, an online nutritional analysis can support participants in maintaining their dietary plan (adherence).
- **Secondary Uses:** Aggregated and anonymized data from online nutrition analysis can be used by the organization (e.g. aggregated BMI – Body Mass Index) to describe the health status from a human capital perspective and to professionalize the overall strategy e.g. in weight management.

However, the **balancing act between feedback and control** must always be observed, as the aim of monitoring is not to incapacitate participants or to monitor them, but to use feedback to enable early risk analysis and awareness-raising among individuals and, from an organizational perspective, navigation towards a healthy organization. At this point, importance should be attached to **informational self-determination** as an essential design principle of IT-based health monitoring and this should be set out in writing in a company agreement (Sect. 3.1). In addition, the involvement of the data protection officer is mandatory.

To ensure that the activity-related volume of data does not become a numbers graveyard from the perspective of the organization, it is necessary to bundle the data streams in the form of a **health balanced scorecard** as a cockpit for the various perspectives of the healthy organization (finances, processes, customers and potentials) (Uhle and Treier 2019).

Digital Evaluation Set of the Healthy Organization
The evaluation set of the healthy organization is based on individual vitality and lifestyle monitoring and, as health controlling, links these data streams anonymously and organization-related with personnel-economic value drivers. The networking by means of IT support is the prerequisite that, despite the extensive data material, the additional effort of an evaluative monitoring is kept within limits and an added value is achieved with regard to the progress of the healthy organization. The virtual health center supports both the acquisition and distribution of information.

3.3 Virtual Health Centre as a Management System

In principle, a corporate health management structure is required from the point of view of process and organizational structure that is compatible with the digital strategy. The framework on which the health center is based is modularized and integrates the fields of action of health management as a networked umbrella strategy.

Modern information and communication technology enables occupational health work to coordinate its various approaches with regard to workplace health promotion, occupational health and safety, operational integration management (return to work), social work or occupational medicine in a **digital ecosystem.** Health is a **concerted action and effort.** CHM 4.0 sees itself as an integration concept, i.e., the goal is not to substitute previous analog approaches in CHM with digital offerings, but rather to implement the overall package according to the target matrix of a "healthy organization"as a **networked platform** based on a sociotechnical system (Connected Health) as part of a digital transformation strategy. *Networking is the claim of an agile health strategy and requires a platform strategy* (Roland Berger 2020).

CHM remains **"physically" anchored** – a detachment from the operational environment is not intended with the digital strategy. Rather, the aim is to create an interface between users and stakeholders that is accessible and also enables decentralized organisational units to participate in the analogue and digital health programme.

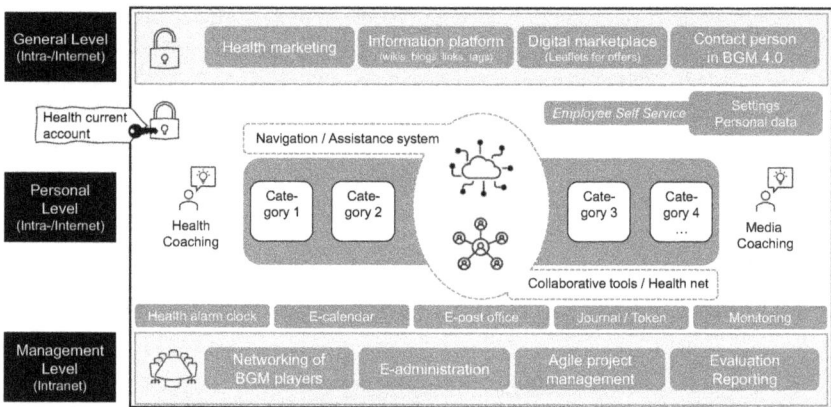

Fig. 3.2 E-building kit as framework CHM 4.0

The virtual health center is based on a flexible, database-driven framework that allows personalization. Figure 3.2 illustrates the **building blocks of the framework.**

The **organizational concept** covers *generally accessible* and *personalized* areas. General information is prominently visible to everyone without access restriction. Personalized services require a login. The health current account as an e-health record contains the key to the virtual health centre (Sect. 3.1). Other **basic building blocks** are …

- electronic transaction processing and ESS module (Employee Self Service),
- collaborative working,
- expert and coaching module as well as the
- digital assistance system as a navigation tool.

The fields of action in the Health Center are categorized according to **content headings** (e.g. exercise, nutrition, stress, recreation, workplace) in the sense of a professional architecture (Chap. 2). Blurring boundaries between the consumer, professional and administrative levels are characteristic of a transaction-centric digital platform. Building blocks for storage (e.g., life cycle, data maintenance), data protection, or electronic mailroom (e.g., signatures) are required. Due to the sensitivity of personnel and health data, these should be integrated with particular care and should always be available as basic modules, regardless of the expansion stage. **Supplementary content modules** such as healthy leadership can be assigned depending on the addressee group. In addition to the basic modules, the virtual health center takes into account a **management and evaluation module.**

The virtual corporate health center has various **expansion stages.** Due to the **modular** structure as a **building block system**, it is possible to successively adapt the underlying infrastructure and the interface to the needs of the organization. However, the technical infrastructure should be planned from the outset with regard to its expandability (horizontal and vertical scalability) in order to meet increasing requirements, e.g. through a larger number of users or more content modules.

In the healthcare market, there are **providers of platforms** that promise effective health promotion, enable management of interventions, make success measurable and ensure compliance with the General Data Protection Regulation (GDPR). If a **full-service provider** is chosen, it should be critically examined in advance whether the platform meets the requirements in terms of data protection, networking and personalization and whether the administration, management and evaluation functions are sufficiently implemented. *Customizing* is usually possible. Quality seals, references and content that meet the prevention guidelines and quality criteria of the GKV (statutory health insurance) help in the pre-selection (GKV 2020) (Sect. 4.1).

The following **variants or expansion stages** are conceivable ...

- Leasing of a health platform with focus on prevention and active courses, which are certified according to § 20 SGB V if possible. Customizing is recommended to increase the identification with the own organization.
- Creation of an own health platform and purchase of building blocks with external quality assurance. Internal control is carried out by the management level.
- Creation of an own health platform as a control centre and production of own prevention and activity modules with internal and/or external quality assurance. This variant allows comprehensive freedom in the design.

The **integrated concept** should link various digital offers of the organization with offers from the private environment in addition to services of the health insurance companies and expand them through collaborative settings (e.g. fitness/work-out challenges such as step competition).

The decisive factor for the success of the integration is the **CHM maturity** independent of the degree of digitalization. The CHM maturity results from the fulfillment of the **quality criteria** based on the minimum standards described in the DIN SPEC 91020, which expires in 2020, on the structure, process and resource level (Kaminski 2013). The effectiveness of digital offerings depends on them being embedded in CHM and legitimized in the system. It is problematic if the digital offerings develop a life of their own. Digital services as surrogates represent a substantial step backwards for quality-oriented, systematic and sustainable health management. The virtual health center is therefore more than a web-based interface for health collections and their administration; at its core, the center functions as a **management model** with the goal of integrating multimodal interventions as a multicomponent program.

A central field of action of CHM 4.0 relates to **management programs** in **CHM** that contribute to the translation of holistic CHM. This key role of the digital transformation of CHM from a management perspective is sometimes neglected in the discourse, as the focus is one-sidedly on digital tools for behavioural prevention (Sect. 4.1). In addition, digital tools in environmental prevention concerning working conditions, such as a risk assessment of mental stress in an online format or a post-field tool for the participatory development of proposals for stress optimization as a learning knowledge system, should also be taken into account (Treier 2020a).

The digital health model is a **mammoth task** in health management, which is best projected as a development assignment. Due to the versatility of the starting points, a management platform is necessary in order not to get bogged down in individual measures (actionism). The **quality management** functions here as a framework for a quality-oriented approach and determines the roadmap to CHM 4.0. For example, reference can be made to the requirements of ISO 45001 as an occupational health and safety management system, which replaces the relevant standard BS OHSAS 18001 (Walle in Matusiewicz et al. 2021, p. 35ff.). The standard elevates occupational health and safety even more to the status of a strategically relevant and mandatory management issue. The focus is on employees and interested parties. The requirements focus on criteria such as work policy, risk identification, risk management and place legal topics in the foreground. An integration of CHM 4.0 into an overarching management system is advantageous, as digital health applications are taken into account in the overall strategy "Healthy Organization", a guideline for implementation is available and certification is made possible.

Management System CHM 4.0
Analogue as well as digital offers need an expert system for coordination and support, regardless of whether the preventive interventions are behavioural oriented or based on the working conditions, and regardless of whether they originate from the organization or from the private environment. In this way, online health coordinators can design tailor-made solutions for individuals and act as a guide in the jungle of offers. A contemporary health platform also includes functions for collaboration, organization, motivation and monitoring. Quality and trustworthiness are the basis of sustainable health management 4.0, which sees itself as a genuine management task.

Success Factors in CHM 4.0

4

The health coach in your pocket, available and accessible everywhere, resource-saving and suitable for everyday use – this could be the recipe for success in corporate health management 4.0 (CHM 4.0). Smart health exercises are not a hurdle in the digital age. But an attractive collection of tools is not enough, because in everyday business life, the conditions such as healthy leadership must also be created so that the digital toolbox is more than just a pretty gadget.

The virtual health center is not just a collection of tools on the intranet or internet as a **digital hawker's tray.** From a quality perspective, independence in terms of time and location, a diverse range of services and personalization stand out as the frontrunners. *But this is not enough.* This chapter discusses the digital toolbox as the nucleon of the health center, self-efficacy as a personal resource, and contextual factors such as healthy leadership as success factors.

© The Author(s), under exclusive license to Springer Fachmedien
Wiesbaden GmbH, part of Springer Nature 2023
M. Treier, *Corporate Health Management 4.0 in the Digital Age*, essentials,
https://doi.org/10.1007/978-3-658-39337-3_4

4.1 Digital Toolbox from a Quality Perspective

The diversity of digital tools in terms of content and format is constantly increasing. The problem is that quality assurance is lagging behind. Therefore, quality is becoming a success factor.

The risk with the toolbox is the **hodgepodge of objects** in the age of the click mentality via app and web. Metaphorically, one can speak of a *digital shotgun* here. The lifestyle and health offerings of the popular app stores illustrate how rapidly and intransparently the digital market for lifestyle, health and medical apps is growing (cf. Bitkom studies, https://www.bitkom.org/). And app hopping is increasing, so that dwell times and expiry times are shortening with implications for their effectiveness, which in turn affects reimbursability. The **digital tangle** is clothed in buzzwords that are under the primacy of technology and at times are off-putting. The diversity in terms of content and format makes it difficult to make a didactically justified selection (content management).

The **range** in the health sector can be illustrated on the one hand as a digital shotgun, but also positively as a digital kaleidoscope. The **selection of digital tools** in the toolbox should not be based on criteria such as modernity or attractiveness, but primarily justified in terms of content (health goals) and reviewed from a quality perspective. The palette ranges from multimedia, learning quizzes, e-coaching, newsletters, Games4Health (gamification), smart textiles, wearables, team events and social media to EAP and age appropriate assistance systems (Ambient Assisted Living, AAL) (Schirrmacher et al. 2018). This list is neither exhaustive nor does it capture recent approaches such as AR (augmented reality), VR (virtual reality) and AI (artificial intelligence) – scenarios that illustrate the trajectory from Web 2.0 (social networking) to Web 3.0 (semantic web) to smart Web 4.0 (artificial intelligence). Cloud-based health services enable networked scenarios. **Limiting factors** include the bandwidth of the Internet, the technical capacity of the end devices, media competence and the technical affinity of the users.

In the health center, low-threshold access to the digital palette should be guaranteed. Due to their flexible use with regard to the wide range of mobile devices, **e-health applications** require a **mobile and responsive design** that adapts to the characteristics of the device. Furthermore, an interface adapted to the needs of the users is expected.

Serious Games or **Games4Health** are the highlight of activating methods to combine health education with fun. However, there is often no real setting and the game level is not classified as serious. Thus, the transferability to real-life settings has to be questioned. Nevertheless, the **door-opening function** has been empirically proven, so that the playful setting can also bring about changes in the real world. The goal is **immersion** as a psychological state, that is to virtually dive in. Virtual reality is perceived as real. There are also intermediate concepts, i.e. real apps with game functions or exer-gaming with physical activation. Almost all Games4Health are behavior-oriented. Design factors are motivation and gratification mechanisms such as digital trophies, the linking of fun and fitness, and competition between peers as challenges. Games are an important pillar of edutainment in health education, in order to overcome one's inner weakness in an entertaining and playful way.

Classification systems from a technical and functional point of view are needed for order (Bertelsmann 2016) (Chap. 2). In order to maintain an **overview,** digital offerings can be divided into five **categories** – often hybrid solutions (Burkhart & Hanser in Matusiewicz and Kaiser 2018, p. 37ff.). E-, M- and P-Health offerings are particularly relevant for CHM 4.0. The categorization illustrates a **paradigm shift,** as static and only receiving approaches are increasingly being replaced by interactive and participatory concepts.

- **E-health** (Electronic Health): Electronically supported activities in the health sector from telemedicine to electronic health cards to health apps as a generic term for digital health tools and services.
- **M-Health** (Mobile Health): Offers for mobile devices as trendsetters in the sense of *"health to go"*, especially health apps with a focus on prevention and active courses (lifestyle apps) using the sensors of the devices (mobile software application).
- **P-Health** (Personalized Health): Digital offers and health services geared to individual requirements as personal digital assistants as well as active participation of users, e.g. in the recording of health data (self-tracking).
- **C-Health** (Connected Health): Sharing personalized health information with health care actors for the purpose of effective counseling and therapy (provider-patient interaction) via group settings to self-help groups in networks.
- **I-Health** (Integrated Health): Collaborative, integrated care that not only targets health promotion and lifestyle, but also takes into account diagnosis, treatment, care and rehabilitation. Integration is seen as a means of optimizing fragmented services to increase quality, effectiveness and efficiency.

As the boundary between work and private life is disappearing and end devices are used in all domains of life from the point of view of M-Health, the question arises as to whether private devices can be integrated into the digital toolbox or whether private equipment from smartphones to apps to networks can be used in the organization (BYOD = Bring Your Own Device). In fact, this can hardly be prevented, but it does pose legal challenges, for example with regard to data protection, liability or questions of employment law. In a virtual health center, a **BYOD concept** is required to define the framework conditions and create legal certainty.

The health care market comprehensively covers all fields of action in health care management with digital services (Chap. 2). Health didactic and health psychological aspects, software ergonomic quality criteria and the guarantee of data protection and data security are to be prioritized in a **quality-oriented selection strategy.** As it is often hardly possible for organizations to define a selection strategy with their own expertise, an **evaluation concept for digital programmes** in the fields of health promotion and lifestyle is needed (Walter et al. 2019). **Quality standards** for CHM online service providers and an overview of the products offered on the market are needed, analogous to the regulatory framework for pharmaceuticals. Many digital applications fall under the headings of lifestyle or wellness, so there are low underlying quality standards here. It is problematic that most health apps do not fall under the Medical Devices Act (MPG), which provides for corresponding tests and controls depending on the classification. Whether a digital health app is to be classified as a medical device depends on whether it meets the definition under § 3 No. 1 MPG.

Software ergonomic evaluations, especially for health portals and apps, refer to the set of rules ISO 9241. The principles of dialogue design and interaction principles (ISO 9241-110:2020) are at the forefront of consideration – these include suitability for the users task, self-descriptiveness, conformity with user expectations, learning facilitation or learnability, controllability, error tolerance or robustness and customizability (suitability for individualization). The basic standard for usability (ISO 9241 T11, quality of use: ISO 25010) stands above these rules. The design aspect of **accessibility** according to the German directive BITV 2.0 (Barrier-free Information Technology Ordinance) must be added.

Various **quality dimensions** must be taken into account in the selection process:

- Content quality (up to date and in line with health science standards)
- Design quality (software-ergonomic, modern and responsive interface, usability)
- Technology quality (data security, data and privacy protection, valid sensors)
- Quality aspects with regard to participants (appropriate to the target group, needs-oriented and personalized)
- Accessibility (e.g. according to Web Content Accessibility Guidelines 2.1)

However, valid information on the offer is often missing; the presentation is primarily oriented towards marketing. Orientation guides are required, but these are hardly available and standardized (Albrecht 2016). The following **quality criteria** help with a pre-selection ...

- *Seal of approval*
  - CE marking according to Directive 93/42/EEC
  - DIN-ISO certification, e.g. ISO 250xx series of standards as benchmark for software development, generally ISO 9001, software ergonomic criteria according to ISO 9241, for medical devices IEC 62304 requirements
  - Based on the guidelines on prevention of the GKV-Spitzenverband (National Association of Statutory Health Insurance Funds)
  - Reference to the Medical Devices Act in the case of medical offers
  - Certification of digital offerings in accordance with § 20 (1) SGB V
- *Competence indicators*
  - Overall portfolio of the provider
  - Competent cooperation partners
  - Membership of associations such as the Society for Prevention
  - Opening up sources of funding
  - Degree of professionalization
  - Publications
  - References
- *Evaluative evidence*
  - Accompanying and external studies
  - Own and external evaluation
- *Content factors*
  - Addressee orientation or target group design
  - Timeliness of health content

- Clarification regarding intended use
- Needs assessment
- Customizing and personalization: tailor-made concepts
- Differentiated didactic formats
- Functionalities with usage restrictions
- Learning and success controls
- Framework plan, target matrix or health strategy
- Participant counselling and coaching
- *Technical factors*
  - Requested rights
  - Documentation system or reporting
  - Feedback options
  - Collaborative work (networks)
  - Modularization
  - Multimedia formats
  - Evidence of data protection
  - Range and accessibility

Quality Oriented Approach
Sluggishness and inertia are at odds with the dynamic digital healthcare market. However, the diversity and intransparency of the offer require a quality-oriented selection. The digital toolbox has a high potential, but often lacks evidence of effectiveness. An evidence-based approach is recommended here. Quality criteria are helpful in creating a framework for the toolbox in the digital chaos.

4.2   Self-Efficacy as a Personal Resource

From a health psychology perspective, self-efficacy is to be promoted and demanded through a digital health model as a personal resource. Empowerment becomes a target value in the health concept.

In CHM 4.0, people are to be empowered to plan their health goals and assess their resources. The **health model HAPA** (Health Action Process Approach) of the health psychologist Ralf Schwarzer (Schwarzer 2004) is suitable as a theoretical framework (Fig. 4.1). Especially in CHM 4.0, the gap between goal setting and

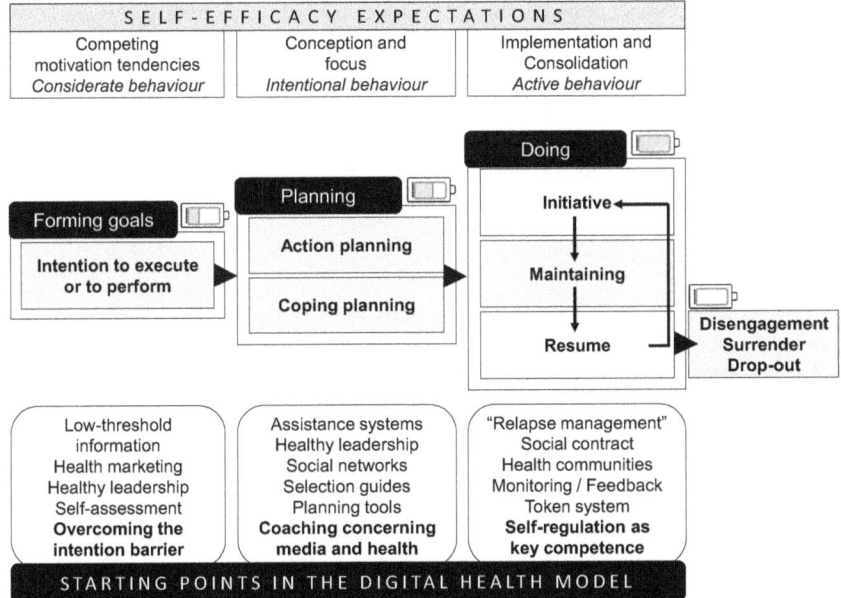

Fig. 4.1 Self-efficacy in the digital health model based on the HAPA model (Schwarzer 2004)

action is relatively large, since the social contract is weaker than in the analogous group setting. The danger of being *"lost in hyperspace"* and thus of **disengagement** are far more likely than in classic offers of CHM. If participants are still motivationally undetermined, health marketing is important to overcome the intention barrier. During the planning phase, targeted information and well-founded support are needed. This is where online coaching can be helpful to avoid misconceptions and misjudgments. During the active phase, feedback can consolidate the health behaviour. In principle, it is recommended to ground CHM 4.0 in health psychological findings already in its concept phase (Knoll et al. 2017).

The more personalized CHM 4.0 is, the more the potential of digital health tools will be exploited (Simmet 2014). **Personalization** contributes significantly to decoding the **DNA of the digital health model**. A *one-size-fits-all approach* does not correspond with the demands of a modern health strategy (Sect. 1.3). Requirements of the life stage and individual settings must be taken into account, because a separation between life domains is inconsistent in the area of health. The more individuals are addressed personally, the more likely they are to be activated. The general goal is to **increase the level of activity.** In this context, **self-efficacy** is the key moderating success and goal factor according to the HAPA model (Knoll et al. 2017, p. 49ff.). It can be postulated that participants with high health literacy and constructive self-efficacy expectations are more likely to perceive and maintain measures even in digital mode (Uhle and Treier 2019). Personal responsibility and participation are pillars in the digital model, but they require **self-regulatory competence** (e.g., ability to defer rewards, mobilize social support, impulse control, or self-critical reflection). If healthy action is unpleasant, it may be postponed until failure.

> **Self-efficacy** refers to the expectation of being able to successfully carry out desired actions oneself on the basis of one's own capabilities. People with high self-efficacy are characterized by a high internal control belief, i.e. they believe that they can specifically influence their state of health. They are less distracted and are focused on the health goal.

Sheldon and Elliot (1999) differentiate four **modes of self-concordance** to be considered in the digital health model with regard to support scenarios, especially when health-related goals are involved.

> **Self-concordance** from a health perspective represents the extent to which health goals correspond to a person's own interests, needs and values. This has implications for the selection, pursuit and achievement of health goals as a regulation of action.
>
> - *External mode:* External reasons motivate involved people to address their health behaviour. Therefore, a digital model should be extended with a token system. The currency of the rewards should generate a health value (double return), i.e. that e.g. new health features are unlocked in the digital tool with engagement. Hidden features are unlocked depending on progress.
> - *Introjected mode:* Here, there is relatively little self-reference, since the participants orient themselves to health authorities ("doctor instructed"). The accompanying coaching in online/offline mode as well as self-assessment tools strengthen the self-reference.

(continued)

(continued)

- *Identified mode:* Participants are intensively concerned with the benefits of healthy action and decide to use the health offers based on rational evaluation processes ("They do sport because it is healthy"). With this group, it is important that the actions in the digital model are sufficiently justified in terms of their effectiveness as a health communication mission. Self-assessment tools can have a positive effect here, as they address the cognitive moment.
- *Intrinsic mode:* Here the action is done for its own sake (autotelic), i.e. one does sport for fun. This group hardly requires any support; on the contrary, the digital model must not be perceived as a disruptive factor. The motivation factor can be strengthened by action-oriented feedback systems.

The degree of the **balancing act between external control and self-control** in relation to health goals depends on self-concordance. The goal in the digital model is always self-control. Therefore, elements that result in external control must not be designed in an intrusive way and should be knowledge-based. The users determine their goals on the basis of measurable parameters and are picked up through challenges and coaching. Expert and evidence-based logics determine the field of action. Planning is done independently by the user. A consolidation of health behaviour can be achieved through social media, competitions and other incentives.

The biggest challenge is **disengagement** or the risk of drop-outs, because many digital measures require a high level of self-regulation competence. Professional **"relapse management"** with follow-up, reporting and proactive coaching counteracts disengagement. Here, impersonal reminders are not enough.

Empowerment and Self-Efficacy
Health apps are attractive to health-conscious employees if they are designed to be convenient and personalized. Self-efficacy is to be increased in digital prevention approaches. However, the premise of high self-regulation competence represents a hurdle, because participants may be overwhelmed with the digital model. Particularly in the digital model, users must not be left alone, but require support depending on the degree of self-concordance. However, support must not be imposed.

4.3   Healthy Leadership as an Organisational Model

The more CHM develops as D-CHM, the more important decentralized (human) support is. Local diversity means adaptation to contextual conditions, and healthy leadership is the extended arm of the digital world into the local organizational unit.

CHM 4.0 can achieve its potential if it has a positive echo in the organization. Many digital programmes are behavioural, but **prevention concerning the working conditions** determines the base on which the digital tools are built. At this point, one could discuss various approaches to the environmental prevention based on working conditions, from workplace design to task design to organizational development, which are linked to behaviour-based building blocks in a prevention matrix (Uhle and Treier 2019) (Chap. 3). In particular, the focus here should be on **healthy leadership**, because leadership is in a balancing act between high performance and exhaustion in the organization.

Healthy leadership links systematic leadership with motivation and participation as well as information and communication. Two perspectives can be defined: health-promoting leadership as a self-management task (self-carefulness) and as a leadership task (carefulness in relation to employees). Managers become prevention managers and promoters of a culture of health.

Confronting the changes in the context of Work 4.0 in a constructive way requires, above all, a new understanding of leadership (Struhs-Wehr 2017) (Sect. 1.2). This is outlined by various technical terms, which have in common that they no longer limit the **role of managers** in the digital age to their hierarchy. Holocratic structures mean that responsibility and decision-making powers are increasingly being handed over to employees. This requires **empowerment as a target variable.**

- *Ambidextrous leadership* describes two-handed leadership on both the economic and human levels.
- *Digital leadership* encompasses the right leadership in Work 4.0 with the success factors of trust, participation, openness and networking.
- *Leadership 4.0* deals with leadership in the digital age and its challenges, from the flexibilization of work to networking and agile working methods.
- *Neuroleadership* addresses needs such as orientation, trust and a sense of purpose. Leaders perceive people cognitively and emotionally.
- *Transformational leadership* calls for value-changing leadership in terms of leading by example, inspiring motivation, encouraging innovation and providing individual support.

Studies reveal that healthy leadership and a healthy leadership culture have positive effects on well-being, commitment and performance and strengthen mental health (Uhle and Treier 2019). Healthy leadership works in sum through small to medium effects and has a high significance because almost all employees have a leader and are thus affected by negative and positive effects of leadership actions (Pundt et al. 2018). From the perspective of the digital health model, leadership can be understood as a **catalyst.**

Many people have a computer workstation. The manager can ensure that ergonomic requirements are met (e.g. height-adjustable desk). Digital instruments such as systems for posture recognition, seat duration detection or digital assistants for adjusting the desk are helpful. However, whether the standing desk actually causes the desired behaviour depends not only on the technology, but above all on the **role model behaviour of the manager** and the activation to use the health-promoting potential of the height-adjustable desk.

Behavioral prevention and prevention concerning the working conditions are intertwined in the digital health model. The digital health model expands the **ability of healthy leadership to act** due to the range, diversity and flexibility of interventions.

The success of the digital approach requires local representation. Managers take on the **role of prevention managers**. They treat themselves and their employees with care in order to be able to meet the challenges of the modern working world with its new forms of stress like mental workload. Healthy leadership requires a health-promoting context (Struhs-Wehr 2017). Four **roles of healthy leadership** can be identified in **the digital model**, which are linked to the bond of trust.

1. *Self-managers:* Consider their own balance between demands and resources, take the role model seriously and convey credibility through self-care (Self Care)
2. *Interaction partner:* Discuss techno/digital stress with employees, take responsibility and communicate health, refer to digital offers, be an online player in social networks (Staff Care)
3. *Resource managers:* Performing a buffer function by allocating resources in Work 4.0 and actively preventing stress, in particular maintaining the digital balance (Supply care).
4. *Work designers:* Design preventive measures of stressful situations with regard to task, environment and organization, e.g. through the use of digital tools, and evaluation through online assessments (Task care).

Increase the Leadership's Ability to Act
Healthy leadership means being a role model, but ultimately also more, because employees expect concrete offers with regard to prevention and health promotion. Digital tools can help to increase the ability of healthy leadership to act, as they offer more options, take local specifics into account and also involve decentralized staff.

Potentials and Risks: A Weighing Conclusion

"Fun, fitness, fascination" could be the success algorithm of corporate health management 4.0 (CHM 4.0), but it must always be remembered in the digital revolution that ultimately real people take care of their health and not avatars. The added value of digital products in CHM is only given if the organization has an activating health culture in which the use of digital interventions is encouraged. It is problematic if digital becomes a fig leaf for doing nothing or for framework conditions that are detrimental to health. Moreover, it must be remembered that there is no medicine without side effects. Consequently, systematic quality control of all digital offerings, from information to communication to transactions, is a conditio sine qua non.

The many advantages of CHM 4.0, such as high reach, topicality and versatility, are offset by concerns regarding data protection, data security and the quality of the offerings. From a health psychology perspective, the digital overload phenomenon is also discussed. Whether the advantages or disadvantages outweigh the disadvantages in the **overall balance** depends on the **implementation strategy** (Chap. 3). The more consistently the implementation is carried out as a *transformation strategy*, the more likely a positive balance is. A strategy that digitally replaces offerings only for efficiency reasons without adapting the framework CHM is problematic.

Table 5.1 compares the **potentials and risks of digital health offerings in CHM** (Albrecht 2016; Schirrmacher et al. 2018). A cost-benefit analysis requires

M. Treier, *Corporate Health Management 4.0 in the Digital Age*, essentials, https://doi.org/10.1007/978-3-658-39337-3_5

Table 5.1 Potentials and risks of digital health offers in CHM

Category	Potential	Risks
Incentives	– Individualized incentives as a gratification concept in analog or digital mode – Integration of bonus systems in e-health tools (token concept) – Intrinsically and extrinsically determined incentive management	– Inducement to extreme behaviour through bonus-malus systems – Danger of instrumentalization of bonus systems as monitoring approaches
Data security	– Data ownership approach – Electronic health record as a precedent – Technical features for data protection (e.g. multi-level authentication) – Avoidance of redundant data acquisition	– Surveillance fear – Big data and cloud as sources of risk – Gateway for cybercrime – Lack of legal regulation – Risk of central storage – Security weaknesses of the terminals – Careless handling of data – Unauthorized disclosure of data – Violation of personal rights
Effects	– Individualization through personalized formats – Impulse generator and catalyst for health behaviour – High update rate – Low deflagration effect due to continuous excitation – No vacuum between interventions – Modularization – Low interference potential (micro formats) – Stimuli through new technical and didactic formats such as gamification	– Increase in the drop-out rate – Attention deficits – Digital stress – The danger of digital self-measurement and self-optimization – Danger of cyberchondria ("Google's disease") – Low emotional attachment – Manipulation by health influencers (persuasion) – Usage and acceptance problems with non-technical addressees – Risks of self-diagnosis – Social isolation – Loss of physical intelligence (body perception) – Orphaned in the digital model ("lost in hyperspace") – Zoom fatigue = online fatigue, hardly any acoustic and media time-outs – Increase in media consumption

(continued)

Table 5.1 (continued)

Category	Potential	Risks
Contents	– Step-by-step approach: From the light to the intensive version, from the layman to the professional – Updating the contents – Holism through linking – Innovation orientation – More diversity in the product portfolio – Low-threshold access – Online consulting concepts – Personalization of the offers – Prevention atlas for all target groups – Psychological issues addressable, less stigmatizing – Extension of analogue offers for deepening	– Absence of the human level – Health information from the internet ("Dr. Google") – Media competence required – Modality of implementation: From dialogic to read-write preference – Staccato approaches ("choppy" health articulations) – Displacement of analogue services
Communication	– Collaborative forms of learning – Modern employer image – Transparent and fast provision of information – Variety of synchronous and asynchronous formats – Desire for increased connectivity in the area of health and prevention	– Absence of social "bodily" control – Prioritization made difficult by diversity (disorientation) – Danger of spam – Inflation of newsletters et al.
Organization	– 24/7 models feasible – Digital administration – No waiting times – Combination with analogue offers – Compatibility with work 4.0 – Avoidance of isolated solutions and offers that are not in line with requirements – Networking with other players as an agile model – Time and location flexible mapping	– Limited control of the offers in terms of professionalism and didactics due to lack of expertise – Lack of interoperability of offers (no standards, compatibility issues) – Self-management (employee self service) as a stress factor – Transferability of the health current account in the event of a change of job – Responsibility diffusion: Self-responsibility principle

(continued)

Table 5.1 (continued)

Category	Potential	Risks
Quality	– Automatic reporting – Accompanying health monitoring – Quality criteria for digital instruments as orientation – Self-tracking – Transparency as a target	– Limited validity of vital sign and activity measurement – Quality deficits due to lack of evaluation of digital offerings – Intransparent and expanding healthcare market – No binding quality criteria (quality seal à la "TÜV") – Hardly any scientific studies on the effectiveness and sustainability of digital offerings
Range	– "Omnipresence" (ubiquitously available in time and space) – Removal of the bottleneck of analogue offers (scalability) – Digital multiplier approaches – Advanced networking – Portability: Not just limited to working life – Target group expansion, including younger and more tech-savvy employees	– Dependence on the presence of functional terminals – Focus on digital natives (Generation Y & Z) – Risk of shifting health promotion and prevention to the private sphere – Risk of discrimination against digital illiterates and non-liners (digital health divide)
Resources	– Decrease in transaction costs – Cloud-based internet solutions – Enhanced quality of care despite cost savings – Low technical costs – Positive cost-benefit ratio – High scalability	– High initial investment, especially in the transformation strategy – Hardly any robust studies on the effectiveness and efficiency of digital interventions – Time and expertise required to select offers
Other	– Anonymity guaranteed – Data sovereignty with the owner – Deregulated concept in CHM – Fit to the digital lifestyle – Positively evolving legislation – Self-determined and responsible health consumers – Linkage with personnel economic drivers	– Legislation lagging behind, but also danger of over-regulation – Self-responsibility as ideology, phrase and fig leaf – How much self-responsibility is reasonable for users?

the consideration of organization-specific parameters (e.g. workforce structure, prevalence of decentralized workplaces, or maturity of the existing CHM). *Fear and euphoria* are bad advisors when deciding for or against a digitization strategy. Many arguments are speculative. However, digital media have in fact changed the way of life. It is therefore important to determine the *how* of digitization and not to discuss the *whether* (Chap. 3). The positive arguments that result from the potentials are to be understood as design challenges. Risks or uncertainties must be countered through participation, transparency and evaluation.

The CHM will profit if analog and digital offers are not placed as competitors, but are built on each other with the determined goal of translating digitization as a mode throughout. **High-performance approaches** are based on networked offerings.

There is no question that anyone who is serious about CHM 4.0 will face **unanswered questions** at the beginning.

- Question about the budget – expenditure of a digital transformation
- Question of participation – readiness and competences of the actors
- Question about previous experience – networks and contacts with providers
- Question of resources – existence of digital content to competence platforms
- Question of cooperation – Stakeholders from occupational health and safety to personnel development to operational integration management
- Question of quality assurance – from operational health controlling to external evaluation
- Question of starting point – pilot or area-wide deployment

To avoid getting lost during the implementation, it is important to define a **roadmap** that is oriented towards quality management (Uhle and Treier 2019). The journey to CHM 4.0 begins with a **target matrix.** Here, emphasis must be placed on the operationalizability of the target indicators, that is, which observable variables (indicators) are to be used to determine the targeted value.

- Addressee orientation (no packaging, tailored programs)
- Increasing attractiveness as a modern employer
- Accessibility
- Data security
- Diversity Conformity
- Increasing self-efficacy as a maxim
- Extension of accessibility (range)
- Coordination of CHM measures (administration, control and evaluation)
- Cost reduction and refinancing options
- Increased sustainability → Transfer to all domains of life (portability)
- Optimization of the individual lifestyle (health behaviour)
- Synergy effects through a mix of analogue and digital measures
- Increase in the level of activity in the prevention fields

In summary, the following **content-related starting points** define the target field of CHM 4.0 (Konnopka 2016; Matusiewicz and Kaiser 2018; Peters and Klenke 2016).

- **Digital administration** of health measures in the field of behavioural prevention and prevention concerning the working conditions and the use of digital management tools for coordination together with the use of digital evaluation instruments. In addition, there is a need for online coaching as a consulting concept.
- **Success factors** from the point of view of practice, such as group settings, use independent of place and time, customizing, etc., are also important. Above all, it is important to increase the everyday competencies of employees in dealing with digital offers in order to enable sovereign health behaviour. Health and media competence must be addressed in equal measure here.
- **Hurdles and risks of digitalization** in health promotion, such as excessive demands on users, handling of sensitive health data, high drop-out rates and the Internet as a danger in the sense of a "source of disinformation" must be taken into account.
- **Legal framework conditions** such as the E-Health Act, BDSG (German Federal Data Protection Act) or DVG (Digital Supply Act). Regulations show the options for using digital tools in the health sector. In particular, the handling of sensitive health data must be discussed here.
- **Relevance and legitimacy** must be demonstrated by evidence of effectiveness, i.e. studies, reviews and meta-analyses, e.g. on the use of digital health apps, but also practical surveys of expectations and acceptance among those affected, in order to develop effective digital concepts.
- **Instruments** ranging from wearables and health apps to EAP-based coaching (e.g. in addiction prevention) are to be integrated into a digital health toolbox. Assessment of the importance of these instruments, derivation of the potentials and risks associated with digitalization, interactions of the tools and evaluation of the combination with analogue approaches are dedicated tasks.
- **Driver factors** such as the flexibilization of the world of work (New Work) or the depth of penetration of digitalization in the domains of life must be taken into account in the CHM 4.0 strategy.
- **Future prospects of CHM** taking into account changes in the working world and technological trends (e.g. virtual reality, game-based health approaches up to the current account health) can be communicated as visions.

Setbacks as *backlashes* in digitization within the framework of a CHM 4.0 initiative represent the greatest danger, because individual deficits sometimes lead to the entire digital model being hastily called into question if, for example, a security leak is identified.

During the **set-up phase,** there will inevitably be competition between modern and conservative products, which will compete and even flirt for the favour of the users. The slogan *"Analog meets Digital"* makes it clear that this encounter in terms of health promotion and prevention is to be determined as an opportunity for mutual enrichment (blended health management). Digital health applications do not make people healthier per se, but they can promote and consolidate health-related activities (adherence). The immense motivation and information potential of digital tools will enrich and transform analogue methods so that the digital moment becomes the **dominant design factor**. CHM 4.0 is currently still to be declared as an innovation offensive. But the emerging normality of the digital transformation ("New Normal") can no longer be shaken – we are becoming more networked, more digital and more flexible – and this also in the healthcare sector. From the perspective of CHM 4.0, this requires a **digital and social responsibility** of the organization (Corporate Social and Digital Responsibility in Healthcare) and not a one-sided shift of health responsibility to the employees in the working world 4.0.

The Digital Upheaval Turns Out to Be More Drastic Than Expected
The digital upheaval in the healthcare sector and in CHM is more accelerated and more radical than expected, as the *"Future of Health"* study manifests (Roland Berger 2019/2020). Therefore, it is no longer a question of cautious probing, but of action, because we are in the fast lane of digitalization. Implementation is often not a question of technology (tool set), but rather of agile behavior and attitude (mindset).

Appendix: What You Can Take Away from This *Essential*

- You will receive general information on the digitization of CHM and the initial situation.
- You will learn about the challenges related to the digital health model.
- You understand the connection between digital health model and work 4.0.
- You will receive a blueprint for structuring CHM 4.0 as a virtual health center.
- You will learn about relevant success and quality factors in CHM 4.0.
- You can weigh the opportunities and risks of digital health offerings in organizations.

References

Albrecht, U.-V. (Hrsg.). (2016). Chancen und Risiken von Gesundheits-Apps (CHARISMHA). Medizinische Hochschule Hannover. https://publikationsserver.tu-braunschweig.de/receive/dbbs_mods_00060000. (Abruf 03/2021).

Altendorfer, L.-M. (2017). *Neue Formate der digitalen Gesundheitskommunikation.* Baden-Baden: Nomos.

Bertelsmann Stiftung. (Hrsg.). (2016). Digital-Health-Anwendungen für Bürger: Kontext, Typologie und Relevanz aus Public-Health-Perspektive – Entwicklung und Erprobung eines Klassifikationsverfahrens. https://www.bertelsmann-stiftung.de/fileadmin/files/BSt/Publikationen/GrauePublikationen/Studie_VV_Digital-Health-Anwendungen_2016.pdf. (Abruf 03/2021).

Cernavin, O., Schröter, W. & Stowasser, S. (Hrsg.). (2018). *Prävention 4.0 – Analysen und Handlungsempfehlungen für eine produktive und gesunde Arbeit 4.0.* Wiesbaden: Springer Fachmedien.

DGB – Deutscher Gewerkschaftsbund. (Hrsg.). (2016). DGB-Index Gute Arbeit – Der Report 2016. https://www.dgb.de/themen/++co++68afe972-a4f4-11e6-8bb9-525400e5a74a. (Abruf 03/2021)

DKV – Deutsche Krankenversicherung. (Hrsg.). (2018). Der DKV-Report 2018 – Wie gesund lebt Deutschland? https://www.ergo.com/de/DKV-Report. (Abruf 03/2021)

GKV – Spitzenverband Bund der Krankenkassen. (Hrsg.). (2020). Kriterien zur Zertifizierung digitaler Präventions- und Gesundheitsförderungsangebote gemäß Leitfaden Prävention 2020, Kapitel 7. https://www.gkv-spitzenverband.de/media/dokumente/krankenversicherung_1/praevention__selbsthilfe__beratung/praevention/praevention_leitfaden/Kriterien_zur_Zertifizierung_digitaler_Angebote_12_2020.pdf. (Abruf 03/2021).

Hackl, B., Wagner, M., Attmer, L. & Baumann, D. (2017). *New Work: Auf dem Weg zur neuen Arbeitswelt – Management-Impulse, Praxisbeispiele, Studien.* Wiesbaden: Springer Gabler.

Haring, R. (Hrsg.). (2019). *Gesundheit digital – Perspektiven zur Digitalisierung im Gesundheitswesen.* Berlin: Springer.

Hurrelmann, K. & Baumann, E. (Hrsg.). (2014). *Handbuch Gesundheitskommunikation.* Bern: Huber.

IFBG – Institut für Betriebliche Gesundheitsförderung. (Hrsg.). (2020). #whatsnext2020 – Erfolgsfaktoren für gesundes Arbeiten in der digitalen Arbeitswelt. https://www.tk.de/resource/blob/2089982/6b926c725e94cff77332e98702d1e835/trendstudie-whatsnext-2020-data.pdf. (Abruf 03/2021).

Käfer, A. & Niederberger, M. (2019). Die Zukunft des digitalen Betrieblichen Gesundheitsmanagements. *Prävention und Gesundheitsförderung, 15* (2), 151–158. https://doi.org/10.1007/s11553-019-00741-4

Kalch, A. & Wagner, A. (Hrsg.). (2020). *Gesundheitskommunikation und Digitalisierung: Zwischen Lifestyle, Prävention und Krankheitsversorgung.* Baden-Baden: Nomos.

Kaminski, M. (2013). *Betriebliches Gesundheitsmanagement für die Praxis: Ein Leitfaden zur systematischen Umsetzung der DIN SPEC 91020.* Wiesbaden: Springer Gabler.

Knoll, N., Scholz, U. & Rieckmann, N. (Hrsg.). (2017). *Einführung Gesundheitspsychologie.* München: Ernst Reinhardt.

Konnopka, T. (2016). Mehr Zugkraft via App und Web: Eine Zukunftsaufgabe im Betrieblichen Gesundheitsmanagement. In M. Pfannstiel & H. Mehlich (Hrsg.), *Betriebliches Gesundheitsmanagement* (S. 327–339). Wiesbaden: Springer Gabler.

Krüger-Brand, H. E. (2019). Digitale-Versorgung-Gesetz: Schub für die digitale Versorgung. *Deutsches Ärzteblatt, 116* (46), A-2111.

Langkafel, P. & Matusiewicz, D. (Hrsg.). (2021). *Digitale Gesundheitskompetenz – Brauchen wir den digitalen Führerschein für die Medizin?* Heidelberg: medhochzwei Verlag.

Matusiewicz, D. & Kaiser, L. (Hrsg.). (2018). *Digitales Betriebliches Gesundheitsmanagement: Theorie und Praxis.* Wiesbaden: Springer Gabler.

Matusiewicz, D., Kardys, C. & Nürnberg, V. (Hrsg.). (2021). *Betriebliches Gesundheitsmanagement: analog und digital.* Berlin: MWV Medizinischer Wissenschaftsverlag.

Million, C. (2019). *Crashkurs Blockchain – Einführung, Grundprinzipien, Use Cases.* Freiburg: Haufe.

Niegemann, H. & Weinberger, A. (Hrsg.). (2020). *Handbuch Bildungstechnologie – Konzeption und Einsatz digitaler Lernumgebungen.* Berlin: Springer.

Otto, Daniela. (2016). *Digital Detox – Wie Sie entspannt mit Handy & Co. leben.* Berlin: Springer

Peters, T. & Klenke, B. (2016). eHealth und mHealth in der Gesundheitsförderung. In A. Ghadiri, A. Ternès & T. Peters (Hrsg.), *Trends im Betrieblichen Gesundheitsmanagement: Ansätze aus Forschung und Praxis* (S. 107–121). Wiesbaden: Springer Gabler.

Pundt, F., Thomson, B., Montano, D. & Reeske, A. (2018). Führung und psychische Gesundheit. *ASU Arbeitsmedizin, Sozialmedizin, Umweltmedizin – Zeitschrift für medizinische Prävention, 53* (Sonderheft), 15–19.

Ramb, W. M. & Zaboroswki, H. (Hrsg.). (2018). *Arbeit 5.0 – oder Warum ohne Muße alles nichts ist.* Göttingen: Wallstein.

Roland Berger. (Hrsg.). (2019/2020). Future of Health 1 & 2. (Studie 1: Eine Branche digitalisiert sich – radikaler als erwartet; Studie 2: Der Aufstieg der Gesundheitsplattformen). https://www.rolandberger.com/de/Insights/Publications/Future-of-Health-Der-Aufstieg-der-Gesundheitsplattformen.html. (Abruf 03/2021).

Schaeffer, D. & Pelikan, J. M. (Hrsg.). (2017). *Health Literacy – Forschungsstand und Perspektiven.* Göttingen: Hogrefe.

Schaeffer, D., Berens, EM & Vogt, D. (2017). Health literacy in the German population—results of a representative survey. *Deutsches Ärzteblatt International, 114* (4), 53–60. https://doi.org/10.3238/arztebl.2017.0053.

Scherenberg, V. & Pundt, J. (Hrsg.). (2018). *Digitale Gesundheitskommunikation – Zwischen Meinungsbildung und Manipulation.* Bremen: Apollon University Press.

Schirrmacher, L., Betz, M. & Brand, S. (2018) Einsatz von digitalen Instrumenten im Rahmen des BGM. In M. Pfannstiel & H. Mehlich (Hrsg.), *BGM – Ein Erfolgsfaktor für Unternehmen* (S. 317–328). Wiesbaden: Springer Gabler.

Schwarzer, R. (2004). *Psychologie des Gesundheitsverhaltens: Einführung in die Gesundheitspsychologie.* Göttingen: Hogrefe.

Selke, S. (2016). *Lifelogging: Digitale Selbstvermessung und Lebensprotokollierung zwischen disruptiver Technologie und kulturellem Wandel.* Wiesbaden: Springer VS.

Sheldon, K. M. & Elliot, A. J. (1999). Goal Striving, Need Satisfaction, and Longitudinal Well-Being: The Self-Concordance Model. *Journal of Personality and Social Psychology, 76* (3), 482–497. https://doi.org/10.1037//0022-3514.76.3.482.

Simmet, Heike (2014). Personalisierung als neuer Erfolgsfaktor in der digitalen Kommunikation. https://heikesimmet.wordpress.com/2014/01/25/personalisierung-als-neuer-erfolgsfaktor-in-der-digitalen-kommunikation/. (Abruf 03/2021).

Social Health@Work. (2020). Eine Studie zur Auswirkung der Digitalisierung der Arbeitswelt auf die Gesundheit der Beschäftigten in Deutschland. Hrsg. von Barmer und Universität St. Gallen. https://www.barmer.de/blob/276178/ea66685b839e7aded009101aa7ba7641/data/dl-studie-social-health-work.pdf. (Abruf 03/2021).

Struhs-Wehr, K. (2017). *Betriebliches Gesundheitsmanagement und Führung: Gesundheitsorientierte Führung als Erfolgsfaktor im BGM.* Wiesbaden: Springer Fachmedien.

TK – Techniker Krankenkasse. (Hrsg.). (2018). Homo Digivitalis – TK-Studie zur Digitalen Gesundheitskompetenz. https://www.tk.de/resource/blob/2040318/a5b86c402575d49f9b26d10458d47a60/studienband-tk-studie-homo-digivitalis-2018-data.pdf. (Abruf 03/2021).

Treier, M. (2020a). Impuls zur gesunden Arbeitswelt: Erfassung und Bewertung psychischer Belastungen am Arbeitsplatz. In V. Scherenberg & J. Pundt (Hrsg.), *Psychische Gesundheit wirksam stärken – aber wie?* (S. 371–398). Bremen: APOLLON University Press.

Treier, M. (2020b). Moderne Instrumente des Gesundheitscontrollings und -Monitorings. Controlling – *Zeitschrift für erfolgsorientierte Unternehmenssteuerung, 32* (5), 26–34. https://doi.org/10.15358/0935-0381-2020-5-26

Uhle, T. & Treier, M. (2019). *Betriebliches Gesundheitsmanagement.* Berlin: Springer.

Walter, N., Scholz, R., Nikoleizig, L. et al. (2019). Digitale betriebliche Gesundheitsförderung – Entwicklung eines Bewertungskonzepts für digitale BGF-Programme. *Zbl Arbeitsmed*, 69, 341–349. https://doi.org/10.1007/s40664-019-00359-5

Werther, S. & Bruckner, L. (Hrsg.). (2018). *Arbeit 4.0 aktiv gestalten – Die Zukunft der Arbeit zwischen Agilität, People Analytics und Digitalisierung.* Berlin: Springer.

ZPP – Zentrale Prüfstelle Prävention. (Hrsg.). (2020). Information für Anbieterinnen und Anbieter von IKT-basierten Selbstlernprogrammen nach § 20 SGB V. https://www.zentrale-pruefstelle-praevention.de/admin/download.php?dl=pruefung_online_angebote. (Abruf 03/2021).